The Southern Guest House Book

Corinne Madden Ross

The East Woods Press

Library of Congress Cataloging in Publication Data

Ross, Corinne Madden.
    The southern guest house book.

    Includes index.
    1. Hotels, taverns, etc.—Southern States—Directories. I. Ti-
tle.
TX907.R589   647'.947503   80-70777
ISBN 0-914788-35-3   AACR2

Cover design by Talmadge Moose.
Inside illustrations and photographs provided by Bill Bradford
and the guest houses of the South.
Typography by Raven Type.
Printed in the United States of America

East Woods Press Books
Fast & McMillan Publishers, Inc.
820 East Boulevard
Charlotte, NC 28203

This book is dedicated to guest house owners—especially to those who have become my good friends.

The Southern Guest House Book

Contents

Introduction

Travelers in Europe have long been familiar with the popular form of lodgings called "bed & breakfast." In the United States, a similar type of accommodation has been available for many years—the guest house, sometimes called a tourist home. Until recently, however, guest houses have received little or no publicity. Now the situation is changing. In some areas guest houses have become virtually extinct, "done in" by superhighways and motels. In other areas the number of houses is on the increase, and more and more of them are following the pleasant British custom of including breakfast in their rates.

The Southern Guest House Book describes more than 70 of these unique establishments, located in Florida, Georgia, Louisiana, Mississippi, North Carolina, South Carolina, Tennessee, Virginia and Washington, D.C. It also includes descriptions of the various states and regions, including their history, and suggestions for places to see and things to do.

If you have never stayed at one, you may be wondering what, exactly, a "guest house" is. It is not an inn, despite the fact that many of the houses call themselves inns, or even hotels in some instances. A true *inn* is a public lodging place that includes a full-service restaurant and usually a lounge or bar. But a guest house,usually, is a private home offering lodging only or lodging plus breakfast.

Guest houses are generally smaller than inns and have fewer rooms for travelers. In most cases the owners live on the premises. Most guest houses are very reasonably priced. Some may still be found that charge as little as five to ten dollars per person per night. Most charge somewhat higher tariffs, and a few are downright expensive; but even the expensive houses are far more modestly priced than most chain motels or hotels. Guest houses are ideal for families, too. Most of them welcome children; their owners will provide cots or roll-away beds for a small fee, and some owners will find a babysitter for travelers. The houses often have porches or pleasant yards or gardens where youngsters can play.

GUEST HOUSES

As a rule, guest houses are conveniently located in or near a town; visitors can easily walk to restaurants, antique and gift shops, museums and other local points of interest. Parking is provided on the premises or nearby. Even if you come without a car, you will be able to get around without much effort.

However, the greatest charm of guest houses lies in their surprising individuality. In the South, their range of architectural styles is as diverse as the region itself. Southern guest houses include stately eighteenth- and nineteenth-century mansions with cool, secluded courtyards; white-columned plantation homes surrounded by extensive grounds; handsome, storied town houses; rambling beach or country farm houses; and even contemporary mountain chalets. Many houses offer a luxurious, old-world elegance seldom found elsewhere today; others are merely simple, unassuming homes providing clean, comfortable surroundings.

A great many Southern guest houses are historic buildings; a number are listed in the National Register of Historic Landmarks and are included on house tours in their locales. Guests in these houses are privileged not only to *see* the houses, but have the added pleasure of *staying* in them.

Guest house interiors may be grand or modest. Many are furnished with lovely antiques. Some have rooms with fireplaces. A number of houses offer entire suites, with sitting rooms and fully equipped kitchens. A pleasant parlor or lounge is usually available for guests, sometimes with a cheerful fire blazing away in chilly weather. Books, magazines, games and television are often provided, too, for rainy days or evening entertainment.

Some thoughtful hosts place fresh flowers or complimentary wine and fruit in each room; others serve afternoon tea or sherry to their guests. If breakfast is included, it may be served on a shady terrace, in the patio, a cozy kitchen or perhaps in a splendidly decorated dining room complete with sparkling chandelier.

Guest house owners, though as individual as their homes, share one delightful characteristic: they truly enjoy their guests and often form lasting friendships with them. You may, of course, have as much privacy as you wish. But if you can, spend some time with your hosts and fellow guests—you will find them interesting, congenial people.

If you stay at one of the South's historic homes, you will probably discover that your hosts have worked hard at restoring the house and will be glad to share their experiences with you.

Ask them, too, for suggestions as to the best places to eat or shops to explore in the area and about local attractions. Guest house owners are deeply proud of their homes and cities or towns and very much want their guests to appreciate them as much as they do.

As guest houses are generally small, with only a few rooms for travelers, it is advisable to make reservations as early as possible via mail or phone. I have listed the latest rates as provided by the proprietors. Prices, however, often tend to increase rapidly nowadays, so it is a good idea to double-check ahead of time. Some guest houses request an advance deposit; a few require a minimum stay (especially during peak seasons). Credit cards are not accepted as a rule; cash or traveler's checks are preferred. Personal checks, too, are often acceptable. There may be a small sales or other tax added to your bill, unless it is already figured in. Tastes vary; so when you arrive, do not be afraid to ask to see the accommodations before settling in. Your host or hostess will be pleased to comply with the request.

Some travelers may find guest houses lacking in certain amenities. Not all offer private baths; in some, guests must share a bath. Many houses do not provide a private phone or television set in each room; there is neither room service, nor an ice machine down the hall. Few visitors, however, find any of these matters an inconvenience or hardship.

I have tried to be as accurate as possible throughout this book, providing as much information as could be gathered about each house. Sometimes, however, situations and/or owners change, and if you should find any of the accommodations described not living up to your expectations, I would appreciate your letting me know. Also, as you will note, there are some areas where guest houses are scarce or seemingly nonexistent. As you travel, if you discover a guest house that you think would make a good addition, tell me about it so that it may be included in the next edition.

For your information, there are two bed & breakfast organizations that offer otherwise unlisted lodgings in many regions of the United States. *The Bed & Breakfast League* has accommodations in Atlanta, Georgia, the Miami/Ft. Lauderdale area of Florida and around Washington, D.C. The League is a membership organization, to which annual dues are paid. Members receive a host directory describing various accommodations from which to choose. For further details, write to: The Bed & Breakfast League, 20 Nassau Street, Princeton,

GUEST HOUSES

New Jersey 08540; or phone (609) 921-0440.

International Spareroom has listings both in this country and in Great Britain. In the South, it includes a selection in Florida, Virginia, North Carolina and Tennessee. The Tennessee listing is an 1835 plantation home that offers guests fox hunting! All include a complete breakfast. The United States booklet, with descriptions of the houses, their locations and prices, costs $1.00. A 50 percent deposit is requested; a three-night or one-week minimum stay is required. Write to: International Spareroom, Box 518, Solana Beach, California 92075, or phone (714) 755-3194.

The American South is a fascinating region, very different from the popular concept of a land held static by its traditions. Today there is a new spirit in the South; lingering nostalgia for grander days has given way to a dynamic upsurge of energy and enterprise evidenced in its booming industry and flourishing agriculture. It is a vibrant, vital region boasting an amazing diversity of scenery, all manner of outdoor activities and sports and a wealth of art, music, and festivals.

Yet respect for history and tradition is strong, and the grandeur of the past has been lovingly preserved. The traveler can still find and enjoy the Classic South—the scent of magnolias, magnificent antebellum plantation homes framed by live oaks festooned with Spanish moss, glorious azalea gardens and historic old towns and cities where a slower, gentler way of life still exists.

The best way to understand and appreciate a region is to get to know its people, and the charming guest houses of the South provide an unequalled opportunity. Without exception, their hosts and hostesses welcome visitors with genuine warmth and interest—and with the South's most outstanding lure, a generous sampling of its fabled Southern hospitality.

Southern Guest Houses

Florida
1. Gainesville
2. Key West
3. Naples
4. St. Augustine

Georgia
5. Columbus
6. Lakemont
7. Milledgeville
8. Mountain City
9. Savannah

Louisiana
10. Jackson
11. New Orleans
12. St. Francisville

Mississippi
13. Natchez

North Carolina
14. Banner Elk
15. Blowing Rock
16. Boone
17. Brevard
18. Kill Devil Hills
19. Minneapolis
20. Nags Head
21. Ocracoke
22. Pinehurst
23. Raleigh
24. Roanoke Island
25. Robbinsville

South Carolina
26. Charleston
27. Mullins

Tennessee
28. Rogersville

Virginia
29. Charlottesville
30. Chincoteague Island
31. Lexington
32. Lynchburg
33. Tangier Island
34. Virginia Beach
35. Williamsburg
36. Winchester

District of Columbia
37. Washington

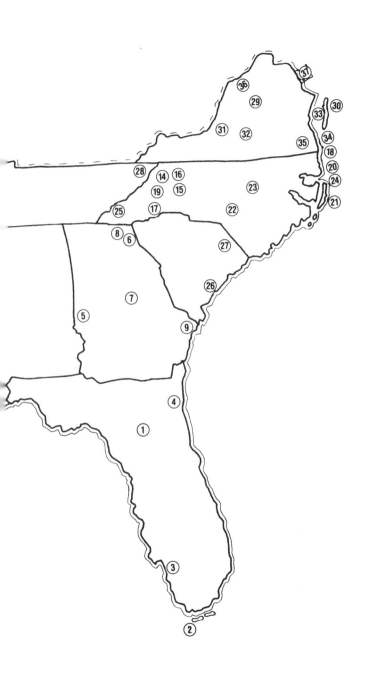

Florida

Florida . . . The word conjures up visions of golden beaches, suntanned bodies and palm trees rattling in balmy sea breezes. Although it has its share of antebellum mansions and Civil War history, it is not really a traditional "Southern" state. Florida is more like a separate world—a water-world, with 8426 miles of tidal coastline, a wealth of crystal springs, 30,000 lakes and great, brooding swamps. It is Disney World, too, and the launching ground for the world of outer space.

More than four and a half centuries ago, the Spanish navigator Juan Ponce de Leon arrived as Florida's first official visitor. In those days, the Spanish were forever roaming around the New World looking for gold (which they often found) and searching for mythical cities and other wondrous fancies (which they did not find). Ponce de Leon, then governor of Puerto Rico, sailed westward in search of a fabled island, which legend claimed held a Fountain of Youth. To the lasting regret of everyone over 40, he failed in his mission. However, he did discover Florida in 1513.

Recognizing a good thing when he saw it, Ponce de Leon claimed the new territory for Spain. Perhaps because he landed during the Easter season (*Pascua de Flores*, the Feast of Flowers), he named the region *La Florida*. After exploring along the coastline, Ponce de Leon returned to Spain and received royal permission to establish a settlement on the west coast. The colony, founded in 1521, did not last long. The local Indians who were not inclined to welcome foreigners, attacked the colony several times. Ponce de Leon and his followers fled to Cuba, where he subsequently died of wounds he had received in an Indian attack. Hernando de Soto and other Spanish explorers also visited Florida in the ensuing years, but hostile natives prevented any further colonization for some four decades.

The arrival in 1564 of French Huguenots, who came to found a settlement near the mouth of the St. Johns River, began a lengthy period of back-and-forth struggles for sovereignty of the

GUEST HOUSES

territory. King Philip II of Spain sent a force to wipe out the French; the French went after the Spanish in revenge. Spain, triumphant for the moment, set up missions in Florida; then the English entered the picture. Sir Francis Drake burned St. Augustine in 1586, and English pirates terrorized the coast in the 1600s. During this era, the Indians were being done away with by practically everyone.

In the early 1700s, English colonists from Carolina burned St. Augustine again, but the Spanish held on. Pensacola, the region's second Spanish colony, was later captured (briefly) by the French. In 1763 Spain gave Florida to England in exchange for Cuba; and during the American Revolution, Florida remained loyal to England. In 1783 Spain got Florida back again, in return for the Bahamas. Twelve years later, Spain sold West Florida to France. (West Florida comprised the southernmost parts of what is now Louisiana, Mississippi, and Alabama, as well as Florida west of the Apalachicola River.) The United States purchased West Florida as part of the Louisiana Purchase. During the War of 1812, Spanish Florida caused the United States a great deal of trouble. Criminals took refuge across its border, and Seminole Indians made frequent raids into Georgia. Also during this time, Spanish rulers were plagued by American settlers in West Florida who declared the independence of the region from Spain. A treaty was finally signed in 1819 in which Spain agreed to turn over East Florida to the United States, and the United States agreed to pay $5 million to American citizens in Florida for property damages.

Florida became a territory in 1822, and large numbers of settlers began to pour in. The U.S. Government confiscated the rich land of the Seminoles for use by the newcomers. For some twenty years bloody battles raged between the Indians and the U.S. military. Most of the Indians who survived were persuaded to move west—all the way to Oklahoma. Florida became a state in 1845 and hoisted its first state flag, a multi-striped design on which was printed in large letters the testy demand: "Let Us Alone." Sixteen years later Florida seceded from the Union, but grudgingly rejoined the United States once again in 1868.

The postwar years were hard ones for Florida; in the latter part of the 1800s and in the early 1900s, however, conditions began to improve. Part of the Everglades was drained, creating new vegetable growing land, and cities and winter resorts sprang up along the coasts. In the 1920s a fantastic land boom developed, only to crash under the weight of the Depression and several deadly hurricanes. Since then, Florida has been on an unprecedentedly stable upswing, based on tourism and new industry.

The state can be divided into four regions: the East Coast, various inland attractions, the Keys, and the West Coast. No point in Florida is more than 60 miles from the sea. On the northeast coast is the charming old city of St. Augustine. Farther south is 23-mile-long Daytona Beach and the Kennedy Space Center on Cape Canaveral. Inland from St. Augustine is Gainesville, home of the University of Florida. Further south inland are Florida's Silver Springs, where visitors can ride in glass-bottomed boats and take a jungle cruise past rhinoceroses, giraffes, camels and other exotic beasts that roam free on the banks of the Silver River.

Walt Disney World and its Magic Kingdom are situated inland, too, west of the Space Center. The 43-square-mile theme park includes six sections: *Main St., U.S.A.*, America from 1890 to 1910; *Fantasyland*, with its 18-story Cinderella Castle and all the beloved Disney characters; *Tomorrowland*, where science fiction comes alive; *Adventureland*, with jungle cruises and "pirates"; *Frontierland*, the American Old (and Wild) West, and *Liberty Square*, a re-creation of Colonial America complete with cobblestone streets. If you are traveling with children, the Magic Kingdom is an absolute must. Even if you're not, go anyway—it is enchanting, spotlessly clean, and appealing to all ages.

Cypress Gardens lies to the south, also inland. The Gardens were once a swamp, but now are a lovely setting for water-ski shows, flowers, canals and rustic footbridges. Back on the East Coast are West Palm Beach, Fort Lauderdale and Miami. In the past year or so, the Miami area has become an enormously popular spot for British tourists, so you may hear the unexpected sound of English accents mixed with those of native Floridians. Lake Okeechobee, a bit northwest of Palm Beach, is Florida's largest lake, a 530-square-mile fishing hole known for its largemouth bass.

The Florida Keys stretch out in a lengthy chain to the southwest below Miami. The Keys are 42 bridge-connected islands between the Atlantic Ocean and the Gulf of Mexico. U.S. 1, a spectacular, toll-free road, goes all the way to the very end of Key West.

Everglades National Park sprawls for some 5000 square miles over the southern tip of Florida. To see it, start at Homestead on Florida Rte. 27, and drive 12 miles southwest to the visitor center. Highway 27, the park's main road, runs for 50 miles to Flamingo. Half land, half water, the Everglades is a unique and magical region of mangroves, mahogany trees, dwarf cypresses, cabbage palms, wild orchids and ferns and watery prairies of needle-sharp sawgrass. Wildlife (not immediately evident, but very much there) includes alligators, deer, bobcats, turtles, fish and birds in a multitude of varieties. Sight-seeing boats embark from Flamingo and also from Everglades City at the northwest corner of the park.

Further on up the West Coast is Naples, a resort community with a fine beach, the African Safari Park and other attractions. The beautiful city of Sarasota, to the north, was once the winter home of the Ringling Brothers Circus. Today Sarasota offers a cluster of circus-oriented museums, including the impressive million-dollar Venetian-Gothic Ringling Residence. Further north are Tampa, with its colorful Spanish/Italian section called Ybor City and Busch Gardens wild game preserve, and then St. Petersburg, where excellent beaches abound.

Weeki-Wachee Spring, about 60 miles north, is another of Florida's magnificent freshwater springs. It produces an incredible 168 million gallons of water each day. Underwater performances of ballet, acrobatics, comedy and tableaux are presented daily at Weeki-Wachee in an auditorium that is itself built under water. (The audience watches the show through thick plate glass windows.)

Tallahassee, Florida's capital, lies a shade inland on the northwest coast, and historic Pensacola is way over near the Alabama border. Both cities combine gracious touches of the Old South with the new Florida. Pensacola includes a spicy dash of Spanish heritage going back to Colonial days.

"The Sunshine State" offers just about everything under the sun to do and see. The Florida State Division of Tourism publishes an excellent vacation guide packed with detailed information. Although visitors flock to Florida each winter, even more come in the summer. Summer weather can be humid, for it rains almost daily, but cooling onshore breezes make visitors comfortable. Native Floridians feel that spring and fall have the most ideal weather. In general, however, Florida is just fine year-around.

ST AUGUSTINE

Ornate wrought-iron gates and balconies, red-tiled roofs and cobblestone streets, Spanish Colonial architecture and horse-drawn carriages ... St. Augustine instantly transports the visitor back in time. And so it should: it is the oldest city in the United States.

When Ponce de Leon reached Florida in 1513, he may well have landed near what is now St. Augustine. Historians are unsure, despite claims to that effect. In any case, King Philip II of Spain later sent Don Pedro Menendez de Aviles to drive French settlers from Florida. Menendez arrived in 1565, led the raid and set up the small colony of St. Augustine.

To consolidate Spanish possession of the territory, the awesome Castillo de San Marcos was constructed in the late 1600s. Indian laborers took 25 years to complete its grim ramparts, dungeons and massive walls. (Some of the walls are 13 feet thick.) The fortress withstood countless attacks and sieges; in later years it served as a British and then an American military prison. Castillo de San Marcos is now operated by the National Park Service. Several times a day visitors can watch the firing of one of the fort's old cannons, a seemingly high-risk process carried out by a person lighting a frayed rope on the end of a very long stick. The flaming rod is then poked gingerly into the cannon as the firer hastily moves to one side.

The flags of Spain, England, the Confederacy and the United States have all flown over St. Augustine. The town, burned and pillaged several times, has miraculously survived with an amazing number of its historical features intact. The Oldest House, dating to the early 1700s, represents several different periods; its site has been in constant use since the early 1600s. The present house, which includes many additions, is constructed of *coquina*, a limestone formed of broken shells and coral. The floors are *tapia*, a mixture of lime, sand and oyster shell.

One of the most interesting sections of the city is *San Augustin Antigua*, a re-creation of the original eighteenth century Spanish village. Restored and reconstructed houses and other buildings, with overhanging balconies and hidden walled gardens, line the narrow byways. Costumed artisans demonstrate their crafts—weaving, baking, candle dipping, silversmithing and the like—in a number of exhibit buildings. St. George Street extends the length of the restoration area, from the old City Gate to the Plaza de la Constitucion with its handsome statue of Ponce de Leon.

GUEST HOUSES

A host of festivals are celebrated in St. Augustine each year, most of them with an authentic Spanish flair. The shrimp boat fleet is blessed on Palm Sunday, and Easter Sunday begins with sunrise services high atop Castillo de San Marcos. In the afternoon the Easter Parade, called *La Parada de Los Caballos y Cochos*, sets forth—with bright Spanish, Indian and American Colonial costumes, colorful floats, bands and decorated carriages. The carriage horses even wear frilly Easter bonnets! In mid-August, the *Dias de Espana*, "Days of Spain," celebration takes place, a three-day carnival honoring St. Augustine's founding. All summer long, from June to early September, an outdoor musical drama called *Cross and Sword* is presented on nearby Anastasia Island.

St. Francis Inn

A.D. 1791

St. Francis Inn, St. Augustine, Florida

St. Augustine is an enchantingly picturesque city of historical sites, museums, and "oldest" buildings, plus a great many contemporary attractions. The best way to appreciate it is to head first to the Visitor Information Center, 10 Castillo Drive, near City Gate. There you can view a movie about the city's more than 400 years of history and pick up all sorts of descriptive material. A leisurely walking tour is recommended, or you may take your choice of a sightseeing train or horse-drawn carriage ride; either one is delightful.

Before you come, however, plan well in advance and make a reservation to stay at the St. Francis Inn. The 190-year-old building has been welcoming guests continuously for 136 years!

St. Francis Inn (formerly Dummett House 1845). This remarkable guest house was built in 1791, as a Spanish home for Senor Gaspar Garcia. It is constructed of coquina, the same material used in The Oldest House, the Castillo de San Marcos, and other ancient buildings in St. Augustine. Between 1795 and 1838 the property changed hands numerous times, but then was purchased by former Colonel Thomas Henry Dummett, an Englishman and native of Barbados.

Dummett had been a wealthy landowner and sugar planter until a slave uprising forced him and his family to flee from Barbados to Florida. After the colonel's death in 1839, his family stayed on; in 1845 his widow, Mary, gave the house to her two daughters, Anna and Sarah. Anna began operating the place as a boarding house, called "Miss Dummitt's" in a guidebook of the day. Another guide, published in 1870, recommended it most highly as furnishing excellent, pleasant accommodations for tourists "at about half the price of the hotels."

In the 1880s the house changed hands again, and the building was enlarged by adding a third story. New owners in 1825 installed central heating, bathrooms, and a lavatory in each room. In 1948 the property was sold once more, and its name was changed to the St. Francis Inn. Mrs. Elizabeth Davis, thirteenth owner/manager of the historic old house, acquired it in 1976 as a gift from her husband.

Restoring and refurbishing the St. Francis were the first items on the Davis family's agenda, but they managed to maintain the house's tradition of never being closed to guests for even one day. Air conditioning was added, and a great many lovely antiques and period pieces. Today the place is a classic example of Old World Spanish architecture and charm. Every room has a fireplace, but no telephone or television set. Guests who wish may watch television downstairs in the old-fashioned parlor. Incidentally, some of the antiques on the first floor are for sale.

The ten guest rooms offer a variety of accommodations, including single and double rooms, two- and three-room suites with kitchenettes, a three-room apartment and a five-room cottage (the former slave quarters). Most accommodations include a living room; all have private baths. The cottage has two bedrooms (each with a bath), a kitchen, living room and Florida room.

Entry to the house is through a courtyard and garden, containing jasmine, bougainvillea, banana trees and other tropical trees and plants. There is even a splashing fountain, and behind a wall, a pool and poolside patio. Guests may also enjoy relaxing on the balcony. Parking is available on a private lot.

The St. Francis Inn is located in the historic section of the city within a short walking distance of The Oldest House and many of St. Augustine's other sites of interest, including the waterfront. No food is served, but there are plenty of good restaurants nearby.

St. Francis Inn, 279 St. George Street, St. Augustine, FL 32084; (904) 824-6068. (Corner of St. George and St. Francis Streets in the Old City, two blocks south of the Town Plaza.) Daily $25 and up, double occupancy; additional persons $5 each; guarantee required with reservation. Discounts for weekly and monthly stays. Cash or personal checks only. Office hours 8 A.M. to 5 P.M. Children are welcome; no pets, please. Open year-around.

GAINESVILLE

Gainesville, seat of Alachua County, was settled in 1830. Earlier, during Spanish rule, much of the area was included in a land grant from the King of Spain to Don Fernando de la Maza Arredondo. Seminole Indian territory bordered the county on the east. When Florida became a United States possession in 1821, the incoming surge of American settlers tried to oust the Seminoles from their land. The Indians resisted removal for a time, starting the second Seminole War (1835-1842).

Today, Gainesville is a peaceful college town, home of the University of Florida. The Florida State Museum, the South's largest museum of natural and social history, is located on the campus. It includes the "Bonompak Room" (a re-created chamber from a Mayan palace), a walk-through forest of 500

years ago, an Indian village, and a fascinating full-size Florida
cave. Gainesville's Morningside Nature Center is especially interesting to children. Its 280 acres of high pine savannas and
sandhills, marshes, cypress swamps and hardwood sloughs form
an enormous wildlife and wild flower sanctuary. Nature trails
and boardwalks provide access into the sanctuary and to "The
1880s Farm," a reconstruction of a typical Florida farm of the
last century.

Thomas Tourist Home. H.D. and Bette Thomas are your hosts
at their seventy-year-old house in Gainesville. It has been a
guest house for 30 years. The Thomases have ten rooms and
three efficiencies available for visitors. The efficiencies each
have private baths; the other rooms share baths. No meals are
served, but there are restaurants within walking distance. Ask
Mr. or Mrs. Thomas to recommend one or two. Parking is
available at the house.
*Thomas Tourist Home, 835 E. University Avenue, Gainesville, FL
32601; (904) 376-9394. Single room $12-$15, double room $15-$18, extra
person in room $5 per night; efficiency $25 per night. Cash only accepted. No pets, please. Open year-around.*

THE FLORIDA KEYS

The word "key" comes from the Spanish *cayo*, or cay, an offshore island of coral or sand. The Florida Keys consist of a
100-mile-long curving strand of some 42 islands, plus a number
of tiny islets and reefs. Thanks to the late Henry Flagler and the
U.S. Government, you can drive all the way from Key Largo to
Key West.

Back in the late 1800s, two forward-looking men, Henry Plant
and Henry Morrison Flagler, brought the railroad to Florida.
Plant built his railroad across the state; Flagler's rolled down the
East Coast from St. Augustine to Key West. Flagler also constructed a string of luxurious resort hotels along the route.
When a vicious hurricane in 1935 destroyed much of the Keys'
section of railroad, the federal government took over the right-
of-way and turned the railroad's path into a roadway, using most
of Flagler's original bridges.

This road is called the Overseas Highway; it is actually an ex-
tension of U.S. 1, which follows along the coast from Maine to
Florida. Considered one of the world's most scenic highways,
the Key road runs between the green waters of the Atlantic and
the blue waters of the Gulf. The bridges connecting the islands

vary in length from about 100 feet to one that is a spectacular seven miles long.

Pirates once used the Keys as a refuge and watering place; Indians found their way here to trade and occasionally to do battle. Several industries brought prosperity to the Keys for a time—cigar making, sponge gathering, and a local effort known as "wrecking" (salvaging wrecked ships and, it is said, sometimes assuring profits by luring the ships onto the dangerous outer reefs). The U.S. Navy, brought in to rid the islands of pirates in 1822, stayed on and made Key West an important military base. The army built a fort here, too. Today the Keys' major businesses are tourism and fishing.

There is an elusive quality to the Keys; old-time inhabitants call it "a state of mind." Life on these remote islands is relaxed and easy going, more West Indian than it is American. The concerns of the mainland seem very far away. This highly individualistic world reflects the tastes of many widely varied types of people and their cultures. Key West, for instance, was settled by a mixture of British, Cubans, Bahamians, Southerners and New Englanders. Key architecture ranges from charming old-world Spanish to contemporary tacky, with just about everything conceivable in between.

For the visitor, there is a wealth of things to do. Boating, swimming, golf, horseback riding and tennis are all available on the Keys, and there are more than 600 varieties of fish. The islands are a bird-watcher's delight, too. For those interested in flora, the Keys offer a tropical paradise of Caribbean pines, breadfruit, Spanish limes, avocado trees, coconut and date palms, pomegranates, oleanders and jasmine.

Collectors of the curious will be intrigued by the several "bat towers" located on the Keys, wooden structures that were built some years ago and stocked with bats from Texas. The idea was for the bats to devour the Keys' mosquitoes. Unfortunately, the notion did not work; the bats apparently preferred their own home-grown insects and immediately flew back to Texas. The towers are still there . . . ask any native to point one out.

Before setting off from Key Largo on the Overseas Highway, pay a visit to the Florida Keys Information Center. Helpful personnel will provide descriptive literature giving full details on the Keys' many attractions and points of interest. Don't miss the John Pennecamp Coral Reef State Park nearby; it runs parallel to the shore and is a 21.5 by 6.5 mile wide underwater park. You can explore the reef in a glass-bottomed boat, or skin or scuba dive for a close-up view of the brilliantly colored living coral and schools of tropical fish. Guides are available for tours.

Further down the chain of islands is Islamorada, known for its superb sportfishing and scuba diving. Children will enjoy Flipper's Sea School at Marathon, where dolphins and sea lions put on regularly scheduled shows. Big Pine Key offers thousands of exquisite orchids at the Summerland Orchid Gardens, and watchful visitors can spot rare white herons and the tiny Key deer on Big Pine.

Finally, there is Key West, southernmost city of the continental United States. (Island and city share the same name.) It is said that human bones were discovered long ago in the mangrove swamps here; "Key West" is actually a corruption of the old Spanish name *Cayo Hueso*, or "bone island." Native Key Westers are known as "conchs" (pronounced konks), named after the ubiquitous local shellfish. The best way to get your bearings is to take a ride on the Conch Tour Train—a one and a half hour narrated tour of the island. Then you can go off on your own, on foot or on rented bike or moped.

Artists and writers have long been attracted to the tranquil beauty of Key West: Ernest Hemingway's home is now a museum open to the public. It is a Spanish Colonial villa made of native stone, set behind a high brick wall amid masses of tropical trees, shrubs and flowers. Here and there and everywhere on the grounds (and inside) you will see cats. There are more than 40 of them, descendants of Hemingway's original 50. Many are double-toed. Cat-loving visitors may, occasionally, adopt one of the kittens. They are free, but only if you promise to send a letter to the present owner of the house each year with a report on the animal's health and happiness.

Also open to the public is the Audubon House, first of Key West's historic homes to be restored. John J. Audubon visited here in the 1830s, and his famed Double Elephant folio *Birds of America* is on display.

At sunset, be sure to head for Old Mallory Square. Key West residents have made a ritual of gathering at the Square at the end of the day to watch the impressive show as the flaming sun seems to plummet suddenly into the western sea. Key Westers are expert judges of their sunsets and award each (according to its merits) with an accolade of respectful applause or (if it's especially noteworthy) loud cheers!

Eden House, Key West, Florida

The Eden House. Mike Eden's delightful guest house was built in 1924. The Gibson family owned it for three generations, operating it as the Gibson Hotel. Mike Eden and his brother Stan bought the place in 1975. They changed its name, but kept the ambiance intact, including high wrought-iron beds and cast-iron bathtubs with eagle claw legs. Straw mats, floral murals, original art and lots of greenery add to the charm. Currently, Mike runs the place and Stan is at school in Michigan, their home state.

The house is the oldest guest house in Key West; it is gleaming white stucco inside and out, with a long ground-floor veranda built out over the sidewalk. There are 31 rooms for guests: 2 singles, 27 doubles, 1 triple and 1 quadruple. Seven have private baths, 14 are semi-private, and 10 are "public" rooms sharing hall bathrooms and showers. All accommodations include in-room washstands. Two of the rooms in the front open onto a second-floor balcony with flowers and hanging plants.

Bermuda ceiling fans cool the individually decorated rooms and the lobby. Guests are invited to make themselves at home in the pleasant lobby and television room, and there are areas for letter writing, games and reading, all with comfortable wicker furniture. A sun deck in the rear is great for tanning or just enjoying the air. No food is served, but below the sun deck is Rich's Cafe, where an array of delectable brunch items is served in a lovely outdoor tropical setting of avocado trees, passion flowers and hibiscus blossoms. Rich's, considered by many to be the best restaurant in Key West, is operated by a friend of Mike Eden's from their college days at Michigan State.

There is plenty of parking available, so you can leave your car and walk, or Mike will rent you a bike. Eden House is conveniently close to Old Town, Key West's historic quarter, several other good restaurants, shops and Mallory Square (for those ceremonial sunsets). Mike Eden says, "The Island is like no other place in America, or the world, for that matter." And he makes a point of telling would-be guests that Eden House is definitely not for anyone looking for typical chain motel accommodations. Instead, guests are offered a very special kind of hospitality—a peaceful, cool, flowery, get-away haven sparked with a distinctive Latin touch.

The Eden House, 1015 Fleming Street, Key West, FL 33040; (305) 296-6868. (Enter the island on U.S. 1, which becomes Roosevelt Blvd. as you turn right. Three traffic lights bring you to Palm Ave.; turn right. Go three traffic lights, turn left, go one light, turn left and pull into parking lot on the left. Or simply ask anyone where Eden House is!) In season (mid-December through Easter): with private bath $32, semi-private $28, bath and shower down the hall $25, plus $5 for additional person. Off season: $16, $18 and $20, plus $5 per additional person. Special weekly and monthly rates are available during the off season. Visa and Master-Card accepted. No children, no pets, please. Open year-around.

NAPLES

If you are driving, getting from the Miami area to Naples on the West Coast is a simple matter. Just follow the historic Tamiami Trail, U.S. 41. From U.S. 1 (south of Miami) pick up Florida Rte. 27 North at Florida City; it connects with U.S. 41, west of Miami. Along the way are Seminole villages, with their raised huts called *chickees*, and sections of the Everglades. Naples, one of Florida's finer resorts, offers a marvelous seven-mile stretch of sandy beach and excellent fishing from its 1000-foot pier. It also has 200-acre African Safari Park and Big Cypress Nature Center. Corkscrew Swamp Sanctuary is a short drive away; here visitors follow a raised boardwalk through the swamp to see some of its thousands of birds, many quite rare. The sanctuary is maintained by the National Audubon Society.

Catherine Tiger, Naples, Florida

Mrs. Catherine Tiger/Guests. This guest house has no name, but it does have a warm and welcoming hostess in Mrs. Tiger. Her pleasant house with white cypress siding was built around 1950. Its ceilings are high, the rooms large and airy. There is a pleasant yard, too, for both sun and shade, with lawn chairs for sitting. Two double rooms with semi-private baths are available for guests, but during the winter months only.

The house is three short blocks from the beach and fishing pier. Several good restaurants are nearby, as are shops and churches. Parking is available. Mrs. Tiger recommends that you leave your car and see Naples on foot or via the very attractive trolley system, "literally a work of art." If you are not driving, she will meet your plane or bus, a gracious courtesy. Guests are encouraged to supply their own breakfast rolls and juice (refrigerator space is available); morning coffee is provided.

Mrs. Catherine Tiger/Guests, 269 Eleventh Ave. South, Naples, FL 33940; (813) 261-8786. (Gulf Shore Blvd., south to Eleventh Ave. South; turn left and go two blocks. House is on the left on north side of street.) (Summer address: c/o J. Nervik, RD 2, Parsonage Lot Rd., Lebanon, NJ 08833.) Rates: $30 a day, single or double; $185 a week. Cash or traveler's checks only. No pets, please. Open December through April.

Georgia

Peaches and peanuts, romantic antebellum mansions and the latest in contemporary architecture, forest-clad mountains, a vast, mysterious swamp, islands and ocean beaches, historic sites from ancient Indian mounds to a twentieth-century President's home—Georgia has them all. The largest state east of the Mississippi, Georgia is an intriguing mixture of the past and present. Its diversity of scenery and wealth of activities offer something for everyone, wherever your interests may lie.

To make traveling through Georgia easy and rewarding for the visitor, the tourist board has divided the state into seven scenic areas: Atlanta, Pioneer Territory, the Northeast Georgia Mountains, the Classic South, the Heart of Georgia, Plains Country and the Colonial Coast. Welcome Centers, strategically located and operated by the state, offer information and an introductory taste of Southern hospitality.

History buffs love Georgia. In the mid-1500s, the Spanish explorer Hernando de Soto sailed to the New World and spent most of the year 1540 roaming the territory now known as Georgia. Spanish missionaries soon followed, setting up outposts in Florida. Meanwhile, the British were busy establishing colonies northeast of Georgia, in the territory called Carolina.

England's King George II, an ever-watchful monarch, studied the situation and spotted possible trouble ahead. Spanish forces could easily move north from Florida to invade British Carolina. Fortuitously, James Edward Oglethorpe, an English philanthropist and prison reformer, wanted to found a haven in the New World for debtors who had been released from British prisons. The King granted Oglethorpe a charter to establish a buffer colony in the region between Florida and Carolina.

In February 1733 Oglethorpe's band of about 120 settlers (including some Europeans fleeing from religious persecution) came ashore near the site of present-day Savannah. Tomo-chichi, the local Cherokee chieftain, sold Oglethorpe some of his land. The colony, named *Georgia* in honor of the king, coexisted more or less peacefully with the Indians for many years.

Between 1738 and 1743, however, the Spanish in Florida did just what George II had feared. They made several attempts to march northward, but Oglethorpe stopped them each time. A man of lofty ideals and adventuresome spirit, he also proved himself to be a fine military leader.

When the colony's charter expired in 1752, Georgia became a royal province. Other settlers soon followed the English—Scot Highlanders, Irish, Welsh, Swiss, German and French. In the tumultuous times of the early Revolutionary War years, sympathies were fairly evenly divided between loyalty to the Crown and the desire for independence. But three Georgians signed the Declaration of Independence in 1775, and in 1788 Georgia became the fourth of the original 13 states.

In the post-Revolutionary period, the state grew rapidly in population. Although its boundaries then extended all the way west to the Mississippi River, most of the region was Indian territory. The increasing need for new land to settle created confrontations, often bloody, with the Indians. In 1802 Georgia ceded all of the area west of the Chattahoochee River to the United States in return for government help in solving the Indian troubles. The Indians were banished, and their hereditary lands were divided among the newcomers.

Back in the 1730s, Georgia had the unusual distinction of being the only colony to forbid slavery. The ban was short-lived for economic reasons and was repealed. Dissension concerning slavery arose again before the Civil War. The pro-slavery faction won out, and in 1861, Georgia seceded from the Union to join the Confederacy. The War devastated the state, leaving most of it in ruins. During the Reconstruction period, however, Georgia began to rise again—literally from the ashes—and embarked upon the upward push that has made it today one of the New South's most prosperous and energetic states.

Atlanta, the capital, is a sophisticated metropolis offering visitors an abundance of entertainment, including fine symphony and theater, art galleries and museums and exciting nightlife. Underground Atlanta, a four-block area of restored 1890-era buildings, now houses shops, boutiques and restaurants—all below street level under a vast viaduct system. Not far from Atlanta (about 16 miles east) is Stone Mountain Park, a 3200-acre recreation area surrounding a great granite monolith, largest in the world. The late President Franklin D. Roosevelt's Little White House and Museum, in Warm Springs southeast of Atlanta, is another popular site for visitors.

Northeast of Atlanta lies *Pioneer Territory*, rich in Indian lore. New Echota, capital of the Cherokee Indian Nation from 1825 to 1838, is located here, as are ancient Indian burial mounds. Chickamauga and Chattanooga National Military Park, the scene of a Confederate victory during the Civil War, is the oldest and largest of the country's military parks. Established in 1890, the park includes the 5400-acre Chickamauga Battlefield. Other sections are just over the Tennessee border.

To the east of Pioneer Territory, Georgia's *Northeast Mountains* include a host of peaks rising more than 4000 feet. Brasstown Bald (4784 feet) is the highest. The region is one of magnificent scenery—mountain views, the Chattahoochee National Forest, lovely lakes for boating, fishing and swimming, and spectacular waterfalls. Tallulah Gorge alone, one and a half miles long with a depth of 2000 feet, has three waterfalls. The movie *Deliverance* was filmed along the Chattooga, one of America's most impressive white-water rivers. If you're traveling with children, they'll enjoy panning for gold at the foot of Crown Mountain, in Dahlonega's Gold Hills.

The region termed the *Classic South* lies southeast of the mountains. Here you'll find Georgia's Confederate past preserved in hundreds of elegant antebellum homes. The town of Washington has more than forty of these serene, white-columned mansions, still lived in today and carefully preserved by their owners.

Westward is the *Heart of Georgia*, including Macon with its beautifully restored Grand Opera House, Fort Valley where most of Georgia's famed peaches are grown and Ocmulgee National Monument. Ocmulgee, the largest archeological Indian excavation in the East, shows the remains of Indian settlements going all the way back to 8000 B.C. Milledgeville offers a driving tour past more than twenty of its historic homes, including the Old Governor's Mansion, a superb example of Greek Revival architecture.

Rural *Plains Country* includes, of course, the small town of Plains—home of our thirty-ninth President, Jimmy Carter. The infamous Confederate military prison of Andersonville is in this region, too. It is a national historic site with exhibits, slide shows and interpretive programs. Callaway Gardens near Pine Mountain has miles of scenic drives, walking trails, a multitude of wild flowers and greenhouses, and even a quail-hunting preserve. Historic Columbus is the site of Fort Benning, the country's largest infantry post.

GUEST HOUSES

Georgia's *Colonial Coast*, about 100 miles in length, is considered by many to be the most intriguing region in the state. It is certainly one of the most diverse. The historic city of Savannah, with its two and a half square miles of restored eighteenth- and early nineteenth-century homes, is where Georgia's Colonial past began. Offshore, a string of barrier islands runs along the Atlantic coast from Savannah south to St. Marys. Cumberland Island, the largest, is part of National Seashore system. Accessible by passenger ferry from St. Marys, the island is an enchanting place of moss-dripping live oaks, saltwater marshes, massive ever-shifting dunes and white-sand beaches. From Brunswick, one can reach Georgia's "Golden Isles," including Jekyll, Sea and St. Simons islands.

The eerie Okefenokee Swamp, "land of trembling earth," lies a bit inland and extends into Florida. Once this 435,000-acre wilderness area was an ocean floor; now it is an enormous freshwater swamp where peat islands float, trembling uneasily at the tread of a foot, cypress trees grow in broad belts, waterlilies bloom in wild profusion and alligators reside in great numbers. From entrances at Fargo, Folkston and Waycross, visitors may explore the swamp by boat.

GEORGIA'S NORTHEAST MOUNTAINS

Once these mountains were accessible only by mule, or—for the hardy—by foot. Cherokee Indians lived and hunted here for centuries. Now travelers may drive through Georgia's mountains on winding roads with dramatic vistas at every turn. The state's only ski resort, Sky Valley, is here, as well as a host of lakes, rugged gorges, covered bridges, apple orchards and the Chattahoochee National Forest.

Visitors may fish, swim, go white-water rafting on the awesome Chattooga River, hike over mountain trails, ride, hunt or golf. Numerous craft shops offer hand-sewn quilts, native pottery and rustic furniture. The hamlet of Helen, an old logging town, has been rebuilt to resemble a quaint Bavarian village with cobblestone streets and many attractive shops and restaurants. Helen's almost year-around calendar of festivals is highlighted by the enormously popular Octoberfest, which runs on weekends from early September to early October. The town of Clayton has a Mountaineer Festival each June, and Dillard presents a Harvest Fair in October to celebrate the region's mountain arts and crafts.

Lake Rabun Hotel. Despite the name, this *is* a guest house—and a delightful one. Dick and Barbara Gray graciously welcome travelers to their rustic mountain home, a two-story stone and brown-stained wood structure on the shore of Lake Rabun, right in the heart of the Chattahoochee National Forest.

Indoors, the focal point of the pleasant wood-panelled lobby is a marvelous stone fireplace; in the evenings and when the air outside is nippy a cheerful, crackling fire warms chilled fingers and toes. The furniture, hand-carved of rhododendron and mountain laurel, carries out the rustic theme.

Most of the sixteen attractively-furnished guest rooms have double beds. One offers three single beds, one has two double beds, and one includes a double bed and two cots. Six rooms have semi-private baths; one has a private half bath; the rest share a bath. Most of the rooms have sinks. The delicious, icy, clear water is from a mountain spring, and the house is cooled throughout by fresh mountain air.

The grounds surrounding the house are wooded, with ferns, mosses and myriads of delicate wild flowers. Dogwood trees, especially lovely in the spring, shade stone paths and sturdy little stone seats provide cool places to sit. Boats may be rented at a nearby marina; a public beach is a short drive away, as are a number of the region's spectacular waterfalls.

The Grays offer guests a help-yourself, complimentary Continental breakfast each morning. Guests are also invited to make use of the picnic area, grill and refrigerator. There's a good restaurant just across the road, and your hosts will be delighted to recommend others in the vicinity.

Lake Rabun Hotel, Lakemont, GA 30552; (404) 782-4946. (Nine miles south of Clayton on Lake Rabun Road. From the south, heading north from Tallulah Falls: turn left at Lakemont at the Lake Rabun sign, approximately two miles from Tallulah Falls, just past the campground on the right. Proceed approximately two miles and turn left at Lakemont Building Supplies on Lake Rabun Road; Lake Rabun Hotel is about two miles further. From the north, coming south from Clayton: turn right at Wiley Standard Station (about 6 miles) on U.S. 441-23. Turn sharp left and proceed approximately four miles. Lake Rabun Hotel will be on your right.) Single $16, double $20; children in same room with parents $4 each. No credit cards accepted; cash only. Accommodations are limited, so early reservations are recommended. A deposit equivalent to one day's stay is required. Pets are discouraged. Open April 1 through October 31.

Lake Rabun Hotel, Lakemont, Ga.

York House. Beautifully situated amidst tall pine trees, York House is a rambling white structure with a long, long double-decker porch. It looks rather like a very large, comfortable farm house. The oldest part of the house—where the owners, John and Mildred Dillon, live—was built as a log cabin in 1865. The guest wing was completed in 1896, and the house (named for its original owner) has provided quiet, tranquil lodgings for visitors ever since. It has long been popular with writers, artists and others seeking a peaceful mountain retreat with a delightful turn-of-the-century atmosphere.

There are twelve guest rooms, including five doubles and seven singles, all furnished in antiques. Ten rooms have private baths; two share a bath. The cool, tree-shaded grounds offer chairs to sit in, and there are picnic tables for outside dining. No meals are served; but a completely furnished, modern community kitchen is available for guests to use, and there are several excellent restaurants within a ten-minute drive. Lakes, a ski resort, scenic mountain drives and hiking trails are also close by.

York House, P.O. Box 126, Mountain City, GA 30562; (404) 746-2068. (Located between Mountain City and Dillard, just off Hwy 441 on York House Road.) Single (one double bed) $13 per night; double (two double beds) $15; extra person in room $1. Cash or personal checks only. Children are welcome; pets are discouraged. Open year-around.

MILLEDGEVILLE

Historic Milledgeville, in "The Heart of Georgia," was laid out in 1803 as the state's fourth capital and still retains its original plan of wide, tree-lined, parallel streets. Some twenty magnificent old homes, circa 1807 to 1879, may be viewed on a driving tour of the city. The Governor's Mansion, built in 1838, served as the home of ten Georgia governors; the handsome Palladian-style structure is open to the public. Also open to visitors is the Old State Capitol building, used from 1807 to 1867. It has been rebuilt and is part of Georgia Military College.

The Bone House. This graciously proportioned structure looks as though it should be included in Milledgeville's famed collection of antebellum homes. It was, however, constructed at a much later date—in the 1950s, by Mr. Frank Bone. Today the house is owned by Martha C. Thornton and her husband.

An imposing edifice, the brick house is fronted by tall,

The Bone House, Milledgeville, Ga.

graceful pillars. The grounds are beautifully landscaped with lawns, trees and shrubbery and lovely formal gardens. Indoors, a free-standing spiral staircase in the foyer first catches the eye. The floors in the house are of six-inch pegged tongue-in-groove oak; the wallpaper and draperies are similar to those selected by Jacqueline Kennedy for the White House.

The Thorntons have five double rooms for guests and provide extra roll-away beds, if needed. Each room has its own private bath and is furnished in antiques. No meals are served; but two kitchens are available for use, and guests are offered complimentary morning coffee. Martha Thornton will be delighted to recommend a good restaurant or two nearby. Ask her, too, for information about a walking tour of Milledgeville's historic section.

Boating and skiing are available in the area, in season, and guests at The Bone House have access to the Milledgeville Country Club for golf, tennis and swimming. Also, Atlanta is only one and a half hours away.

The Bone House, 529 W. Hancock Street, Milledgeville, GA 31061; (912) 452-5676, 452-2214 or 746-8643. (Located four blocks west of center of town on Ga. 49.) Single or double $35 per night. Cash or personal checks only. No pets, please. Open year-around.

COLUMBUS

Columbus is sometimes called "the fountain city"; fountains seem to be everywhere—in public parks, beside office buildings and on residential lawns. This very attractive city has broad, tree-shaded streets, many fine old homes and a marvelous outdoor historical museum, the Chattahoochee Promenade. The promenade, which runs along the banks of the Chattahoochee River, was developed as Columbus' permanent observance of the nation's Bicentennial. It ties together such local points of interest as the Confederate Naval Museum, Oglethorpe Monument, Amphitheater, Bicentennial Plaza and the old Columbus Ironworks.

Visitors may also follow the Heritage Tour, which includes the Springer Opera House (a restored Victorian theater where Edwin Booth once performed) and several historic houses. At Fort Benning nearby, the U.S. Army Infantry Museum offers displays tracing the evolution of the infantry from the French and Indian Wars to the present.

The De Loffre House

The DeLoffre House, Columbus, Ga.

The DeLoffre House. Situated on a brick-paved parkway in Columbus' Historic District, Shirley and Paul Romo's elegant home is a restored 1863 townhouse in the Italian style. One of its early owners was William L. Tillman, president of the Merchants' and Planters' Steamship Line.

Each of the four luxurious guest rooms has its original fireplace and is decorated in lovely antiques. Each room has its own private bath, phone and color television. One room has twin beds, one has two double beds, and two have one double bed.

Charmingly Victorian though it is, DeLoffre House offers guests every modern convenience. In addition, the Romos thoughtfully furnish each room with a decanter of sherry and a bowl of fresh fruit. In case a traveler has forgotten to pack an item or two, the rooms also contain a shaver, shampoo, shower cap, and books to read! A complimentary Continental breakfast of juice, homemade date-nut bread and coffee is served on antique china, accompanied by a newspaper, in the handsomely appointed, candlelit dining room each morning between 8 and 10 A.M.

Parking is available at the rear of the house. The Chattahoochee Promenade, Convention Center and old Ironworks are only a block away. Several fine restaurants and historic Springer Opera House are also within walking distance. And a short drive will take you to Plains, Georgia, President Roosevelt's Little White House in Warm Springs, Callaway Gardens, Providence Canyon, Lake Eufala or Fort Benning.

The DeLoffre House, 812 Broadway, Columbus, GA 31901; (404) 324-1144. Single $42.50; double $49.50; each additional person in room $7. MasterCard, Visa, American Express and personal checks accepted. No pets, please. Open year-around.

SAVANNAH

General James E. Oglethorpe was an amazing man. He founded the colony of Georgia in 1733, offered a new life to English debtors and to persecuted religious dissenters from Europe, fought off invading Spaniards, and created America's first planned city.

Savannah, first capital of Georgia, sits atop a high bluff overlooking the Savannah River. Oglethorpe's original design for the city was a spacious, symmetrical system of houses and garden plots interspersed with handsome public squares and green parks; the plan is still considered worthy of imitation by urban planners. Although a few of the 24 old city squares were razed in earlier, more callous times, a 2.5-square-mile area has been named a Registered National Historic Landmark. It encompasses more than 1100 architecturally and historically important buildings, 1000 of which have been restored.

From its beginning, Savannah has been a thriving seaport with a fine, deep-water harbor. Long ago its waterfront was lined with wharves and warehouses, seamen's taverns and inns and was a rowdy hangout for sailors and pirates. Today a multimillion-dollar revitalization of the waterfront area has turned the old cotton warehouses into boutiques, studios, museums, quaint taverns and restaurants.

In 1778, during the Revolutionary War, the British captured Savannah. A year later French and American forces tried to retake the town, but were defeated at a ghastly cost—Count Casimir Pulaski and 1700 of his men were killed during the siege. In 1782 General "Mad Anthony" Wayne finally drove out the British. In the Civil War, Savannah was blockaded by the Union Navy. General William T. Sherman ended his march to the sea here in 1864. Rather than risk the total destruction suffered by Atlanta, Savannah surrendered on December 22. General Sherman then sent his famous message to President Lincoln: "Sir, I beg to present to you as a Christmas gift, the city of Savannah with 150 heavy guns and plenty of ammunition and also about 25,000 bales of cotton."

Although Savannah did not suffer the devastation that other Southern cities sustained in the Civil War, the twentieth century brought its own form of destruction. Large sections of the city deteriorated and were razed, in the name of "progress." Some of its loveliest old homes were lost forever. But in 1955 the Historic Savannah Foundation was formed, and since then the city has dedicated itself to an ongoing program of restoration and preservation.

Savannah is a "walking" city; both the Historic District and waterfront can best be appreciated when explored at a leisurely pace. Begin by dropping in at the Visitors Center, 301 West Broad Street, where you can see a slide presentation of the Historic District and pick up rafts of informational material.

For those who do not wish to walk, there are driving and bicycling tours (you may even rent a cassette player and descriptive tape at the Visitors Center to take along with you), and guided bus tours. Most fun of all is to take a carriage ride in an authentic, restored antique carriage with your own coachman to tell you about Savannah and its history. Boat cruises of river and harbor are also pleasant ways to observe the city from a different viewpoint.

Throughout the year Savannah offers a broad variety of special events. In March more than 20 privately owned historic houses and gardens are opened to the public for daylight and candlelight tours; in April there's a walking tour of private gardens. The Savannah Arts Festival is presented in May. In June nearby Thunderbolt celebrates the Blessing of the Shrimp Fleet with street dances, pageants and parades. And these are only a few of the goings-on. During the Christmas season a whole array of holiday observances takes place: candlelight tours of homes, Christmas concerts, carolers and even a traditional British Yule feast.

Savannah has a unique, virtually irresistible charm. It is a combination of many things—streets shaded by majestic oaks, parks and lush gardens, a glorious collection of classic houses, a fascinating waterfront, old forts, history galore, fine Southern food and inhabitants who very much want to share their beguiling city.

Among Savannah's most attractive features are her guest houses. Although these homey establishments are dying out in many regions, in Savannah they are, happily, on the increase. Most of them are in the Historic Section and have their own lengthy histories, distinguished architecture, working fireplaces and secluded, brick-walled courtyards. Making a choice of which house to try may be your most difficult decision during your stay. Of course, you could plan to remain indefinitely and experience them all. As one proud citizen says: "Savannah is so interesting and beautiful, there is no need to go elsewhere!"

Mary Lee, Guest Accommodations. Only a few years ago Savannah had no guest houses at all. Then hospitable, friendly Mary Lee, a native Savannahian, decided to offer a portion of her home to overnight guests. Other house-owners soon followed suit, but because Mary Lee was the first, it is only right that her charming accommodations should lead the list.

Mary Lee thoroughly enjoys the experience of running a guest house: "I've had the fun and the feeling of accomplishment in restoring my carriage house and furnishing it for visitors, and now I have the pleasure of sharing it with some of the nicest people anyone could ever hope to meet. Guests have come from all over the United States and Canada, as well as England, France, and even South America . . . and they've all been pleased (both with their lodgings and their location) and vowed to come back again for another visit and to send their friends as well."

Mary Lee's home is a four-story, tabby-over-brick row house. Built in 1854, it is located in the heart of the downtown Historic District. She has three complete and separate apartments for overnight (or longer) guests: one is on the ground floor garden level of the main house, and two more are in the restored carriage house.

Each apartment consists of a living room, bedroom, kitchen and bath. They are ideally suited for couples, but families can be accommodated. Children are most welcome; Mary Lee is herself the mother of three. One apartment has a double bed, one has twin beds and a queen-size sofa bed, and the third has twin beds plus a day bed that sleeps one. The rooms are furnished with a nice assortment of period pieces such as an iron bed, pine chests and tables, oak and wicker furniture, lots of pictures and baskets and a variety of small "collectibles." There are also plants and fresh flowers, and at the foot of each bed is a handmade quilt.

Mary Lee furnishes free coffee and juice for each apartment and there is usually a bowl of fresh fruit on the table in each living room. Each apartment kitchen has its own dishes, glasses, pots and pans, silverware, paper plates and cups.

Guests enter through an iron gate at the front of the house; the old carriage house is in the rear beyond the courtyard. Now a walled garden, the courtyard is ideal for enjoying morning coffee or a cocktail on a warm spring day. In summer months there is almost always a cooling breeze, especially in the late afternoon and evening.

Private parking is not available, but on-street parking is plentiful. Mrs. Wilkes' famous boarding house restaurant is just down the street, and just about everything visitors want to see or do in Savannah is within walking distance. Be sure, while you are there, to ask Mary Lee to tell you more about her interesting house. For instance: when the original walls were gutted during restoration by a previous owner, two Civil War swords were discovered. There is an opening in the floorboards in the main house that was apparently designed as a hiding place for valuables. And although she has never seen it, Mary Lee says there once was an entrance under the carriage house to an underground, brick-paved tunnel that ran under the back lane.

Mary Lee, Guest Accommodations, 117 East Jones Street, P.O. Box 607, Savannah, GA 31401; (912) 232-0891. Daily rates are $40 per unit, but will most likely increase $5 or $10 in 1981. Special monthly rates are available, particularly during the winter months. Cash or personal checks accepted; no credit cards. Open year-around.

The Stoddard Cooper House 1854. A four-story townhouse, the Stoddard Cooper House was originally built for a plantation owner who often traveled to Savannah to conduct his cotton business. Located on Chippewa Square in the heart of Historic Savannah, the house changed hands many times and was even a shop for a while. In 1977 David and Barbara Hershey bought the place. The Hersheys came to Savannah from Buffalo, New York, a move brought on partly because of the great Buffalo blizzard of '77. Relocation in a Southern city with more moderate weather seemed like an excellent idea, and Barbara, who had visited Savannah 20 years earlier, was interested in the city's restoration program.

The old house they chose was in sad shape. Although the Hersheys had to gut the building, they managed to preserve its classic high ceilings, fine crown moldings, medallions, Savannah gray bricks, heart pine beams and much more. Visitors are invited to see the restoration, still in progress, and hear the stories of some of the trials and tribulations involved in the massive undertaking.

Guests are accommodated in a luxurious ·two-bedroom garden suite. (If only one bedroom is booked, the other is left vacant, not rented to another party.) The layout consists of one bedroom with king-size bed and one with twin beds, plus a large (1500 square feet) living room, a full bath and completely equipped modern kitchen. It is ideal for a family or for two couples traveling together. A baby crib can be supplied if needed. The living room was the house's original kitchen and boasts an enormous wood-burning fireplace. There is another fireplace in the bedroom and fires are laid ready to light when guests arrive. The rooms are all tastefully furnished with American antiques and wicker, and handmade quilts.

A free Continental breakfast is provided: fruit juice, rolls, jam, butter and coffee are in the suite's refrigerator ready for guests to serve themselves. Also included is a welcoming bottle of wine. For an extra charge, the Hersheys will cater meals for guests. The brick-walled sunken garden with lush tropical greenery is available for guests to use, too, for having refreshments or just for sunning and sitting. Parking is available.

The Stoddard Cooper House 1854, 19 West Perry Street, Savannah, GA 31401; (912) 233-6809 or 234-5305. Rates are $48 to $78 nightly, $300 to $425 weekly, $1,000 to $1,500 monthly. A 30 percent deposit for reservations is requested in advance; cash or check, no credit cards. Open year-around.

"Four Seventeen," The Haslam-Fort House. Alan Fort, convivial host that he is, is one more new-come Savannahian who is in love with his adopted city and its treasures. As he says: "Most Savannahians are walking Chamber of Commerce addicts in their own right, and I seem to fall into the same category. Forgive me, but it's infectious!"

"Four Seventeen" is located in the landmark district, within a ten-minute walk of most of the city's other historic highlights. A three-story brick town house in the Italianate style, it is unusual in that it does not have a high stoop entrance to the parlor floor. There is a full side yard (garden) on the property, also rare for Savannah town houses.

The house was built in 1872 for John Haslam, an independent entrepreneur who produced minstrel shows after the Civil War. Haslam was unfortunately lynched in a town in Ohio when he angered an eager audience by failing to put on the show. Although he succumbed in Ohio, his ghost (so says Mr. Fort) still resides on the third floor of his Savannah house (once a Savannahian always a Savannahian) and can occasionally be heard stomping around in the late evenings. He and Mr. Fort are, you'll be glad to know, quite friendly due to their mutual love for the house.

Guests stay in a garden suite, which has two bedrooms, a spacious living room with fireplace, a full kitchen and bath. The high-ceilinged, airy rooms are furnished with antiques mixed with comfortable miscellany. The accommodations are suitable for a couple, a family or two couples traveling together. Cribs and baby-sitters are provided if requested. The suite, centrally air conditioned and heated, is entirely separate from the rest of the house and comprises the entire garden floor. Entry is to the west of the house through the garden, which guests are encouraged to use. Free parking is provided in the lane directly behind the house.

Coffee, tea, Sanka (and a coffee maker), orange juice, English

"Four Seventeen"
417 East Charlton Street
Savannah, Georgia 31401

muffins, bagels and cinnamon buns are provided free on a self-serve basis. The suite's refrigerator also holds complimentary soft drinks and a bottle of wine. The kitchen is equipped with pots and pans, dishes and silverware; so you may cook in or, if you like, Mr. Fort will suggest a caterer.

Alan Fort, a former actor and New York advertising account executive, speaks German, Norwegian, Spanish and some French. He acts as a concierge for his guests, arranging reservations for dinner, theater and tours, and is eager to help you in every way possible to thoroughly enjoy Savannah. He will even sell you a house if you decide to stay permanently! (Mr. Fort is also a real estate agent.) He is an avid toy and doll collector, too; be sure to ask him to show you his collection.

Pets are allowed, within reason. Two dogs (Maude and Rhonda) and one cat (Myrna) live in the upper part of the house. It is their territory, so take your chances. No chimpanzees, please! *The Haslam-Fort House, 417 East Charlton Street, Savannah, GA 31401; (912) 233-6380. (Between Habersham and Price Streets, adjacent to Troup Square.) Single or couple nightly $58, weekly $375, monthly*

GUEST HOUSES

$1,250. Three persons nightly $68, weekly $425, monthly $1,350. Four persons/family nightly $78, weekly $450, monthly $1,450. (All plus 7 percent hotel/sales tax.) One night's deposit required for a stay of two or more nights; $25 deposit required for one-night stay. In the event of cancellations, deposit will be carried over to a future booking as a credit. Discount of 10 percent given to senior citizen couples on a stay of three days or longer if requested in advance and with proper identification. Local telephone service, television and radio provided; weekly maid service provided with long-term stay. All utilities are included. Cash or personal and traveler's checks preferred. Open year-around.

Liberty Inn, 1834. Frank and Janie Harris may well be the busiest couple in the South, let alone in Savannah. Not only do they own and operate the guest house called Liberty Inn, they also maintain two Savannah restaurants—the Regency and the Shrimp Factory!

The Harrises welcome visitors to their restored nineteenth-century three-story home in the Historic District; they offer four exceptionally attractive suites for guests. The house, a survivor of the many devastating fires that swept over Savannah in earlier times, is clapboard over brick, Federal style. Colonel William Thorne Williams of the Chatham Legion of Militia built the place; he served six terms as Mayor of Savannah and was also a publisher and bookseller. During the late 1800s and under different ownership, the house was one of the town's major social gathering places. In the 1930s the building became a rooming house and cafe, then was abandoned. The Harrises purchased it in 1967.

In restoring the house, Frank and Janie carefully preserved the original brick fireplaces, exposed beams and interior brick walls. Each guest suite is painted in Historic Savannah Tabby White, one of the colors commonly used in the city's Colonial era. The rooms, all different, are furnished with comfortable brass beds, period pieces and antiques. Paintings and fresh flowers add to their appeal, and the Harrises have placed books on Savannah's history in each room for visitors' enjoyment.

The suites, all on the house's lower level, are thermal-sound insulated with individually controlled air conditioning, private phone, and color cable television. All but one have a working fireplace. There are two two-bedroom suites and two with one bedroom, all with extra sofa beds. Each includes a family/sitting room, kitchen, modern bathroom, ample closet space, wall-

Liberty Inn, Savannah, Ga.

to-wall carpeting and a laundry center with washer and dryer. The all-electric kitchens include dishwashers, utensils, dishes and flatware.

Your hosts provide a complimentary Continental breakfast: you'll find English muffins, orange juice, butter, preserves and cream in the refrigerator in each suite, to go with your coffee whenever you want it.

Every suite has its own private entrance to the large, semi-enclosed, landscaped courtyard, which is yours to enjoy. There is even a Jacuzzi whirlpool bath and spa, a hot tub and a gas-fired grill. Parking is available for five cars.

The Harrises are a mine of information about Georgia's history and legends. Ask them to tell the story behind Chatham Artillery Punch, Savannah's most noted drink. The punch is a concoction of catawba, rum, gin, brandy, Benedictine, whisky, strong tea, brown sugar, orange and lemon juice and cherries. And that's only the base. Champagne is added just before serving.

Liberty Inn, 1834, 128 West Liberty Street, Savannah, GA 31401; (912) 233-1007. Prices range from one couple at $65 per night or family of four at $75, to $80 or $90 for the larger suites. Group rates are available upon request. Major credit cards are accepted. No dogs, please. Open year-around.

GUEST HOUSES

Eliza Thompson House. Yet another of the lovingly restored old Savannah homes is the Eliza Thompson House, presently owned by Laurie and Jim Widman. The house was built of stuccoed brick in 1847 for a "ravishing redhaired widow," Eliza Shaffer Thompson. It was the first town house erected in the city's most fashionable section, Monterey Ward; Mrs. Thompson lived in it until her death in 1875.

The Widmans have preserved the house's original heart pine floors and many fireplaces, including one that measures an impressive six feet by six feet and was originally used for cooking. Restoration is still continuing, and the number of suites available for guests is increasing from five, each with private bath and entrance, to a possible 18. Each large suite accommodates two or more people, and every one has a different decor.

Most suites are elegant in style, with oriental rugs and historic print fabrics; one (the suite with the enormous old cooking fireplace) has a cozy country look, with gingham, eyelet embroidery and hooked rugs. Laurie Widman provides thoughtful extra touches, such as silk flower arrangements in baskets or porcelain and beautifully patterned percale linens; soap and color-coordinated face cloths and towels are neatly rolled up in baskets. Each room includes at least two genuine antique pieces, but the beds have new, custom-made firm mattresses. Suites all have air conditioning, private sitting rooms and television.

Each kitchen or kitchenette is kept stocked with a complimentary Continental breakfast to be eaten at the guest's convenience. And a crystal decanter of sherry on a silver tray graces each suite, plus two beautifully illustrated books on Savannah. The Widmans have named each of their five original suites for a Savannah great. The history of each person, copied in exquisite calligraphy on parchment, has been framed and hung.

The Eliza Thompson House is a very intimate kind of guest house; it offers today's comforts combined with the graciousness of the nineteenth century. Guests are invited to use the parlor front porch (with wicker and director's chairs and lots of green plants) and the pleasant back yard garden, too. Pets are allowed, but please inquire first. "Mannerly children are welcome," Laurie Widman states. "We have two youngsters of our own." Private parking is available at the house.

Eliza Thompson House, 7 West Jones Street, Savannah, GA 31401; (912) 236-3620. (At the corner of Jones and Bull Streets.) Singles begin at $35;

Eliza Thompson House, Savannah, Ga.

deposit required. If guest stays for seven days, the eighth day is free. Rates include daily maid service. Cash, personal or traveler's checks accepted; no credit cards. Open year-around.

GUEST HOUSES

Chippewa Inn. The Chippewa, a handsome, Venetian Revival-style house, is located in the exact center of Savannah's Historic District on Chippewa Square, the largest of the city's Colonial squares. The mellow tones of its brick facade are typical of Old Savannah. Constructed in 1895, the four-story house was purchased in the late 1970s by Robert Cornwall, an ex-resident of San Francisco. Now restored, the Chippewa offers two single and four double rooms with semi-private baths. Complimentary morning coffee is provided, and parking is available.

Bob Cornwall will graciously direct guests to Savannah's multitude of shops, museums, restaurants, old forts and other historic sites.

Chippewa Inn, 14 West Hull Street, Savannah, GA 31401; (912) 233-2416. Single $20, double $30; cash preferred, no credit cards. No pets, please. Open year-around.

Remshart-Brooks House. Martha Brooks, another of Savannah's boosters, is your hostess in this lovely nineteenth-century home. Lived in by the same family until just a few years ago, it is part of Remshart Row, which was built in 1854. Mrs. Brooks says: "We welcome guests into our home so that we can share the complete renovation. . . . Our courtyard is walled and perfect for early morning coffee or afternoon tea after a day of seeing Savannah. Both rooms in our garden apartment have working fireplaces with a supply of wood for an evening by a cozy fire. There's color cable television, too, plus a well-stocked library for our guests to enjoy, including many books on Savannah."

The garden suite consists of one large bedroom with queen-size bed, a dining/living room with double sleeper sofa, completely equipped kitchen and bath. A baby bed is available for small children. The fireplaces are of beautiful old brick; the comfortable, attractive furnishings are perfectly appropriate to the period, and plants here and there add a cool touch of greenery.

Off-street parking is provided, as is a complimentary Continental breakfast of coffee, tea and orange juice, always available. Remshart-Brooks House is directly across the street from Mrs. Wilkes' famed eating establishment. (Mrs. Sema Wilkes has been serving breakfast and lunch to Savannahians and visitors since the 1940s in old-fashioned boarding house style—everyone sits together, and the food is served piping hot

Remshart-Brooks House, Savannah, Ga.

from large dishes set in the center of the table. The cooking is renowned, incredibly reasonable, and impressive in quantity.) Ask your hostess, Martha Brooks, to tell you more about the place.

Remshart-Brooks House, 106 West Jones Street, Savannah, GA 31401; (912) 236-4337. (If you are driving: On I-16 take Exit 37B to Montgomery Street to Liberty, turn right to Whitaker Street—one way going south—and turn right onto West Jones. The Remshart-Brooks House will be at the second set of steps from Whitaker.) Rates: $40 per night per couple, $50 if additional person. MasterCard and Visa, personal checks or cash accepted. No pets, please. Open year-around.

The Palmer House. This newer guest house is located in Ardsley Park, a beautiful residential section of Savannah five minutes from the Historic District. Betty M. Palmer purchased the house in 1977; it was built in 1921. The large apartment for guests offers a bedroom with king-size bed, private bath and cooking facilities and a fireplace in the sitting area. A greenhouse on the premises keeps the rooms supplied with fresh flowers, including orchids! The suite is furnished with antiques and original paintings.

A charming brick garden walk leads to the guest quarters, and there is an enclosed patio for outside dining or sunning. A Continental breakfast of juice, coffee and sweet rolls is provided, plus a complimentary bottle of wine. Mrs. Palmer also plans to offer lunch and/or dinner to guests in the near future, if requested in advance. Parking is available; restaurants and shops are minutes away by car. Palm tree lined Victory Drive, leading to the beach road (a twenty-minute drive) is two blocks away.

The Palmer House, 519 East 45th Street, Savannah, GA 31405; (912) 233-2969. Rates: $40 per night, cash or personal checks accepted. No pets, please; infants, but no young children. Open year-around.

Louisiana

Beautiful is the land, with its prairies
and forests of fruit-trees;
Under the feet a garden of flowers,
and the bluest of heavens
Bending above, and resting its dome
on the walls of the forest.
They who dwell there have named it
the Eden of Louisiana.

These lines may not be as familiar as "This is the forest primeval . . . the murmuring pines and the hemlocks," but they are part of Henry Wadsworth Longfellow's narrative poem *Evangeline*. And for many travelers, Louisiana means "Evangeline country," that region of the state where Acadian exiles settled after being driven from their Canadian homes in the eighteenth century. Although Longfellow created his own romantic version of the tragic exodus, the basic tale is a true one.

Acadia, now Nova Scotia and New Brunswick, was first settled by French colonists. It later became a British possession. In 1755 the British ordered the Acadians to renounce their Roman Catholic faith and swear allegiance to the Crown. They refused, so were dispossessed of their land and dispersed to various sites, including New England, France and the Indies. Some of them made their way to Louisiana. Although the region was under Spanish rule at the time, the Spanish authorities welcomed the new arrivals and gave them grants of land.

That new world must have seemed incredibly exotic and strange to those weary emigrants from far-off Canada. In Louisiana the Acadians found a semi-tropical region of great rivers and sleepy bayous, marshes, mysterious cypress swamps, and rich, fertile soil. Different though it was, the hardworking, deeply religious newcomers adapted quickly to their new surroundings and soon became valued members of the colony. Between 1765 and 1788, many more Acadians came to Lousiana;

their descendants, some of whom still speak an intriguing mixture of French and English, live there today. They are called *Cajuns*, a form of the word Acadian.

There is of course a great deal more to Louisiana than its fascinating Acadian heritage. The French influence is very strong; Louisiana was originally settled by colonists from France in the 1600s. The following century brought not only the Acadians, but also French aristocrats fleeing both the Revolution and slave uprisings in the West Indies. The French Napoleonic Code, rather than Common Law, is the basis of law in the state. Eighteenth-century Spanish Colonial influence, too, may be seen in many of New Orleans' old structures with their lacy ironwork, and Spanish is still spoken in some areas of the state. Descendants of the early French and Spanish settlers are called *Creoles*. Counties in Louisiana are known as *parishes*, a custom going back to Spanish rule.

English planters settled much of the region east of the Mississippi and north of Lake Pontchartrain; German pioneers emigrated here in the 1700s, making their homes along the Mississippi and in North Louisiana. Much of the state's distinctive cuisine and its jazz heritage came with black slaves from Africa. After Emancipation, free blacks in Louisiana amassed large holdings of land. Italians, Irish, Yugoslavians and Hungarians have also made their own ethnic contributions to the state's colorful blend of traditions and culture.

Seven governments have ruled all or part of Louisiana: the French, the Spanish, the English, the Republic of West Florida, the Republic of Louisiana, the Confederate States of America and the United States. The tangled tale began with the Spanish adventurer Hernando de Soto back in the 1500s. De Soto, like many explorers in those days, was searching for another golden empire similar to the Incas'. He did not find it, but he did discover the Mississippi River in 1541. In 1682 Robert Cavelier, Sieur de La Salle, voyaged down the Mississippi and laid claim to the region in the name of France. La Salle named it *Louisiana*, for the French monarch Louis XIV. The first permanent settlement was established in 1714, at Natchitoches; New Orleans was founded four years later.

In 1763, by the Treaty of Paris, France ceded Louisiana west of the Mississippi (plus New Orleans) to Spain, and the region east of the river (except for New Orleans) to England. The English ruled their section, called the *Florida Parishes*, until it became part of Spanish Louisiana in 1781. In 1800 Spain ceded to France all of Louisiana except the Florida Parishes, which were part of the region known as West Florida. And in 1803 the United States clinched one of the biggest real estate deals in our history—the Louisiana Purchase.

President Thomas Jefferson bought the vast Louisiana Territory from Napoleon Bonaparte for fifteen million dollars. The almost one million square miles of new land later became part or all of the states of Louisiana, Missouri, Arkansas, Iowa, Minnesota, North and South Dakota, Nebraska, Kansas, Oklahoma, Wyoming, Montana and Colorado.

The Florida Parishes section, however, was still owned by Spain. Then in 1810, a band of American settlers staged a rebellion and captured Baton Rouge. They established the independent West Florida Republic, but 90 days later joined the American Territory of Louisiana. Louisiana became a state in 1812 and was admitted to the Union. It seceded in 1861 to become an independent republic—for 55 days. Then Louisiana joined the Confederacy and, after the Civil War ended, was readmitted to the Union in 1868.

NORTH LOUISIANA

North Louisiana is typically Deep South, with many antebellum homes and several Civil War battlefields; it is a lovely, rural land through which runs the Red River. An enormous log-jam called the "great raft" once blocked the river for about 180 miles. In 1835 a riverboat captain named Henry Miller Shreve (later the founder of Shreveport) invented an ingenious "snagboat." He battered a channel through the woody debris, opening the river upstream from Natchitoches for navigation. Shreveport is a thriving city; it is the home of the Louisiana State Fair, held each October, and also of the famous country music show *Louisiana Hayride* (Elvis Presley got his start there). Flower lovers should not miss the American Rose Society Gardens nearby, a 118-acre expanse of roses and camellias. There is Fort Humbug, too, where Confederate forces tricked enemy scouts by placing charred logs to look like cannons.

Natchitoches (pronounced Nak-e-tash) lies to the southeast of Shreveport; it is the oldest settlement in the Louisiana Purchase Territory. Roque House Museum, a rustic 1803 plantation building, offers a fine example of a French Colonial house with its mud, moss and cypress-beam construction. At the Natchitoches Parish Chamber of Commerce Tourist Commission nearby, visitors can pick up a map of the area's historic sites and other points of interest. And for an entertaining lesson in local history, try to see *Louisiana Cavalier,* a lively outdoor musical drama. It tells the story of the French explorer Louis Juchereau de St. Denis, who founded Natchitoches in 1714, and depicts his struggles to establish friendly relations with the Indians and Spanish. The play is presented on weekend evenings between late June and late August.

ACADIANA

Now we come to Evangeline country, known as Acadiana. It is composed of twenty-two parishes that form an enormous triangle in Southwest Louisiana. Here the unique Cajun culture is everywhere—in the language, the music, the cuisine and the people. Fishing and fur trapping are still major occupations along the region's rivers and bayous; Louisiana leads the country in fur production. The town of Lafayette is considered the unofficial capital of Acadiana. There you can visit the Acadian Village and Tropical Gardens, five miles south, to see what an early Cajun bayou village looked like. The village includes a number of restored houses and other structures and splendid gardens.

Longfellow's poem was based (very loosely) on a supposed real-life romance between two young Acadians—Emmeline Labiche (Evangeline) and Louis Arceneaux (Gabriel). In historic St. Martinville not far from Lafayette, the Evangeline Monument marks the grave of Emmeline Labiche. And the ancient Evangeline Oak is said to be where her boat docked at the end of the long journey from Novia Scotia. St. Martinville was settled by Acadians in the late 1700s' during the French Revolution Royalist refugees from France arrived and turned the village into a miniature version of Paris with their grand balls, operas and other elegant events. The Petit Paris Museum contains a fine collection of furniture, Mardi Gras costumes and other artifacts once owned by the aristocratic French settlers. At the Longfellow-Evangeline Commemorative Area near town you can explore the Acadian House Museum. Supposedly, the eighteenth-century building once belonged to Louis Arceneaux, Evangeline's beloved Gabriel. The grounds, on the bank of Bayou Teche, are lovely.

ST. FRANCISVILLE/JACKSON AREA

East of Acadiana on the other side of the Mississippi is Baton Rouge, Louisiana's capital. Be sure to see the impressive State

Capitol Building; from its observation tower there is a
marvelous view of the city and surrounding countryside. Other
interesting sites to visit are the Old State Capitol, the old and
the present governor's mansions, the Louisiana State University campus and the Greater Baton Rouge Zoo. The name *Baton
Rouge*, by the way, means "red stick." According to the records
of early French explorers, long ago a post—probably a red
cypress—marked the boundary between the lands of two Indian tribes.

Louisiana has some sixty plantation mansions and
antebellum homes open to the public. Their wide range of architectural styles reflect the tastes and backgrounds of their
original owners. The mansions are scattered throughout the
state; so as you travel, inquire at the local tourist headquarters
for detailed information and directions on how to reach them.
North of Baton Rouge (about 25 miles), the area around St.
Francisville offers an array of impressive plantations. And St.
Francisville itself is a delightful old village set high on a hill by
the winding Mississippi River.

Rosedown Plantation is a beautifully restored example of
antebellum opulence (located half a mile east of the town on
Hwy. 61 and Hwy. 10). In addition to a magnificent oak alley
(avenue), there are 28 acres of gardens with flowers, greenery,
ornamental statuary and charming gazebos. The mansion, built
in 1835, contains a wealth of paintings, murals and antique furnishings. The Myrtles (one mile north on Hwy. 61) is of French-
style architecture and was constructed in 1795. It is highlighted
by a 110-foot-long gallery.

Catalpa (four and a half miles north on Hwy. 61) is a
reconstruction of the original plantation house, which burned
shortly after the Civil War. A pleasant late Victorian home filled
with family treasures of five generations, it is situated in a
parklike setting of 30 acres of gardens.

Oakley Plantation (four miles south of St. Francisville on
Hwy. 61 and then left on Hwy. 965) includes a 100-acre
Audubon Wildlife Sanctuary. John James Audubon lived at
Oakley, a West Indies-style house, and painted many of his
famous "Birds of America" here. Rosemont, Jefferson Davis'
boyhood home, is further out (about 25 miles north of St. Francisville).

These are only a few of the area's collection of historic sites.
Some of the plantation houses and their grounds are open year-
around, others only in season or by appointment. Ask at the

GUEST HOUSES

West Feliciana Historical Society Museum in St. Francisville for details.

Several of the region's plantations and historic houses also offer overnight accommodations for guests, and staying at any one of them is guaranteed to be a memorable experience. One establishment is in St. Francisville itself, another is just outside the town, and there are two more in Jackson, a few miles east.

Propinquity. Listed in the National Register of Historic Places, Propinquity is a handsome brick house owned by Charles and Gladys Seif. Built by John Mills in 1809, the structure was enlarged in 1816 and restored in 1966. It is the oldest house in St. Francisville, located right in the center of the village. Between 200,000 and 300,000 bricks were used in the construction of the place, which has in its time served as a bank, a boarding house, an apartment house and (twice) as a private residence. The historic house is included on the Audubon Pilgrimage, a special tour of homes and gardens held each March.

Generally, there is one suite available for visitors; it consists of a large sitting room, a master bedroom and a modern bath with tub and shower. The tub is one of those delightful old-fashioned ones, and the furnishings are all late nineteenth-century Louisiana antiques. For couples traveling together, a second double bed is available.

Guests are invited to make use of the wide gallery (porch) that runs the length of the house. And Propinquity's grounds are something special—about four and a half acres of lawns and gardens with camellias, azaleas and many other kinds of flowers, plus pecan and fig trees. During the fall and winter months when the leaves are off the trees, there is a lovely view of the Mississippi. Plenty of parking is available on the premises, in the large back yard.

The Seifs pamper their lucky guests with a delicious complimentary Continental breakfast, which includes Propinquity Jam Cake (the house specialty), coffee, tea or milk, and homemade preserves. Breakfast is even brought up to your door, at whatever time you request. For other meals, ask Mr. or Mrs. Seif to recommend a good restaurant or two. They will also be pleased to tell you how to reach some of the other historic houses in the area. And Mrs. Seif will graciously provide you with a copy of her recipe for that delectable Jam Cake—a lasting souvenir to take home and re-create in your own kitchen.

*Propinquity, 523 Royal Street, P.O. Box 814, St. Francisville, LA 70775;
(504) 635-6855. (Located in the center of town, corner of Johnson and
Royal Streets.) Rates: $35 double occupancy including breakfast; second
double bed in room $35 extra per night. Rates subject to change without
notice. Cash, personal or traveler's checks accepted; no credit cards. Please
make reservations in advance, at least a week ahead. Rooms will be held
only until 4 P.M. unless advised of late arrival. No pets or children. Open
year-around except Christmas and New Year's.*

The Cottage Plantation. One of the few complete antebellum
plantations remaining in the South, The Cottage is located on
Hwy. 61 just north of St. Francisville. Included on the plantation are the main house (with accommodations for guests) and a
large collection of outbuildings: the old schoolhouse, kitchen,
milk house, carriage house, barn, slave quarters, commissary,
smoke house and others.

At first glance the low, rambling, two-story main house looks
rather like an English farm cottage, but with an exceptionally
long front gallery. Actually it is a series of buildings joined
together, erected between 1795 and 1859. The earliest part of
the house was designed in the Spanish tradition with square,
airy chambers, each opening onto a gallery through tall door-
windows. The transoms also exhibit the Spanish influence with
their delicate, curving fretwork. The tall blinds have stationary
slats; these were installed to thwart the local Indians' inquisitive
nighttime habit of prowling around outdoors and peering in at
the inhabitants.

The last section of the house to be built was the 65-foot-long
great wing. Its front gallery adjoins the back gallery of the
original building. Except for the massive poplar sills, The Cottage was constructed entirely of virgin cypress. All the woodwork inside and out and the galleries' pillars are hand wrought.
Each room in the house has a hand-carved fireplace mantel;
some extremely elaborate, others quite simple.

The plantation's land was originally a Spanish grant acquired
by John Allen and Patrick Holland. Thomas Butler purchased
the place around 1811. Butler, a native of Pennsylvania, moved
first to the Mississippi Territory, then to Louisiana where he
later served as a state congressman and judge for many years.
Butler died in 1847 and is buried here, in a small walled
cemetery on the grounds. A number of famous people have
been guests at The Cottage, including Andrew Jackson. He

Cottage Plantation House, Saint Francisville, La.

stayed here en route to Natchez shortly after the Battle of New Orleans.

Mr. and Mrs. J. E. Brown are now the owners of The Cottage Plantation, and your gracious hosts. They cordially invite travelers to come and stay awhile and experience a taste of plantation life as it was long ago. Five double rooms and one single room are available for guests, some with double beds, some with twin beds. All have private baths, and are air conditioned. The house is furnished throughout with antiques; many of them date back to the Civil War era and even earlier.

Outdoors, from the south galleries, you look out at the old plantation buildings. From the north gallery you will see a woodland of ancient live oaks adrip with Spanish moss, magnolias, poplars, beeches, hollies, crape myrtle, dogwood and evergreens. Fenced English gardens at the ends of the long galleries boast superb azaleas and Japonicas—over a century old, and tall as large trees. Beyond are green pastures; the tiny old cemetery lies at the edge of one of them. A contemporary addition to the plantation is an outdoor swimming pool. The old plantation kitchen is now an antique and gift shop. Parking is available on the grounds.

The rates include coffee delivered to each room at 8 A.M., breakfast served in the dining room, and a tour of the entire house, outbuildings and grounds. The Cottage Plantation, by the way, is registered as a National Historic Site and is on the list of famous houses in the area to be toured.

The Cottage Plantation, Rte. 5, Box 425, St. Francisville, LA 70775; (504) 635-6374. (On Hwy. 61, 5 miles north of St. Francisville, at Cottage Lane.) Rates: $40 per couple per night including breakfast and tour. Cash or checks accepted. No pets, please. Open year-around, except Christmas.

Milbank House. Located in Jackson, Milbank is an absolutely elegant nineteenth-century Greek Revival town house. Long galleries in the front and back are graced by large Doric columns; the front gallery shades three French doors and matching walk-through windows. The rear gallery also offers a cool, shady place to sit where one can look out onto a large back yard of huge trees, some of them 200 years old.

The site was once owned by the founders of Jackson, John Horton and R. Ficklin. It is believed that the house was built by Hezekiah and Elizabeth Keller in 1836; later it was sold to the president and director of the Clinton and Port Hudson Railroad Company for a banking house. The building has also served as a hotel, boarding house, dance hall and apothecary shop.

Today Milbank is a private residence owned by Neil and Carol Hunter, with one guest room for travelers. The home is beautifully furnished in antiques and some reproductions; it is open to the public for tours, and guests are given a personal tour. The Hunters and their family live on the upper floor of the house. Downstairs there is a large side entry hall with a handsome curving staircase, a parlor, dining room, kitchen, powder room and the guest room with private bath. A large double fireplace serves both parlor and dining room. The guest bedroom, adjoining the parlor, includes a rice-carved four-poster bed among its other lovely nineteenth-century antiques.

Guests are invited to enjoy a large, complete breakfast served each morning in the dining room with its stunning crystal chandelier. Breakfast is included in the rates. Parking at the house is available; restaurants and antique shops are within walking distance. For a change of pace from touring planta-

Milbank, Jackson, La.

tions, the Audubon State Park, five miles away, offers picnic grounds and hiking trails.

Milbank House, Box 905, Jackson, LA 70748; (504) 634-7273. (On Bank Street, half a block south of Hwy. 10.) Single $25 per night, double $45 per night, including breakfast and house tour. Extra person using roll-away bed, $5. Cash, personal or traveler's checks accepted; no credit cards. No pets, please. Open year-around.

Asphodel Plantation. Asphodel is not a guest house, strictly speaking, but rather a complex of old and new buildings that include accommodations for guests. The plantation encompasses the main house, a number of outbuildings, including guest quarters, shops, an inn (now serving as a restaurant), a barn and lots more. On the extensive grounds are a swimming pool, two stocked ponds, a couple of rambling creeks, the old family cemetery and beautiful woods for walking or bird-watching.

Benjamin Kendrick began construction of the original house in 1820. *Asphodel*, in Greek classical legend, meant a flower resembling the narcissus. The Elysian fields were said to be covered with asphodels, and Kendrick felt that he had found his own "Asphodel Meadow" here in Louisiana. John James Audubon visited the place in its early years and painted por-

70

traits of Mr. Kendrick's daughter and her two sons. When Kendrick died, his daughter married the new owner, a Mr. Fluker. They furnished the house with antiques brought back from their travels in Europe.

Then came the Civil War. Mrs. Fluker, then a widow, confronted the Yankees as they spread out from the Battle of Port Hudson in search of food. Once during a raid, she and her children locked themselves in the library while the house was set afire. Fortunately, the flames died out and the place was spared. In later years, Asphodel became the property of two spinsters, the Misses Smith. In all their years they never left the grounds; when they died in the 1940s, they were buried here. The John Felzers bought Asphodel in 1949 and carefully restored it to its original beauty. Then Felzer died, and the house was purchased in 1958 by its present owners.

Your hostess is Mrs. Marcelle Reese Couhig, and Asphodel offers ten rooms for guests, with more planned for the future. The accommodations all have air conditioning, heat and private baths; they range from four rooms over the gift shop to several large, separate cottages. The cottages, surrounded by huge pine trees and flowering dogwood, have bunk beds for children and separate bedrooms for adults. When making a reservation, specify your needs for twin or king-size beds, small suites, etc. Extra roll-away beds are available, too. Parking is available on the premises.

A full country breakfast is included in the rates. The plantation also serves lunches and dinners (extra, of course) with a tempting selection of such good things as Crab Corn Soup, Red Beans and Rice with Ham, Shrimp Creole and Seafood Gumbo, Crawfish Etoufee, "Coq-au-vin and Dirty Rice" and such luscious desserts as Trifle and old-fashioned Lemon Pie. The bread, made right there, is famous.

Asphodel Plantation, Rte. 2, Box 89, Jackson, LA 70748; (504) 654-6868. (Near Jackson on Hwy. 68 north, off Hwy. 61 toward Natchez.) Rates: $30 single, $40 for two persons, $45 for small suite, $7.50 each for extra person in room—all including full breakfast. Visa and MasterCard accepted. No pets, please. Open year-around except Christmas Eve and Christmas Day.

Another of Louisiana's famous plantations, Oak Alley, may be visited on the way to New Orleans. Leaving the St. Francisville/Jackson/Baton Rouge area, take Interstate 10 northeast to Rte. 22 and across Sunshine Bridge to Rte. 18. The plantation is situated between St. James and Vacherie. Back in the early 1700s an unknown French settler built a small house on the site of the present mansion. He planted twenty-eight live oaks in two well-spaced rows reaching from his house to the Mississippi. The quarter-mile alley of oaks is now more than 250 years old. The magnificent Greek Revival mansion was built between 1837 and 1839 by Jacques Telesphore Roman, a wealthy French sugar planter, for his new bride. In 1925 Andrew and Josephine Stewart purchased Oak Alley, which had fallen into disrepair. It became the first of the Great River Road plantations to be renovated and today is considered one of the finest examples of adaptive restoration in the region. Oak Alley may be toured year-around except Thanksgiving, Christmas and New Year's Day.

NEW ORLEANS

It is virtually impossible to find anyone who has been to New Orleans and has not fallen in love with the place. The city's reputation for superb food, fascinating architecture and classic jazz is well-deserved. New Orleans is one of America's most picturesque and cosmopolitan cities, with an ambiance distinctly its own.

It is an old city within a new one, a very *large* city that is full of *little* places. Despite its size, there is a sense of intimacy. New Orleans is a city of neighborhoods, of narrow streets and byways, of charming gardens and hidden courtyards. Its French and Spanish heritage is very much in evidence even today in its old, historic buildings, its food, and its customs.

Although first explored by a Spaniard, Louisiana was originally settled by the French. New Orleans was founded in 1718 by the governor of the Louisiana colony, Jean Baptiste Lemoyne, Sieur de Bienville. Lemoyne named it for the Duc d'Orleans, then regent of France. In 1762-63, however, France ceded Louisiana to Spain and England, and New Orleans became a Spanish possession. The town's French citizens were not at all happy over that turn of events and for a brief period tried to overthrow Spanish rule. Then in 1800 New Orleans was ceded back to France in a secret treaty; twenty days later (to the shocked chagrin of the inhabitants) France sold the city along with the rest of the Louisiana Territory, to the United States.

During the next few years, Americans came to New Orleans in large numbers, doubling the population and bringing in needed money. In 1812 the city became Louisiana's capital; it remained so until the seat of government was moved to Baton

Rouge in 1880. The British attacked New Orleans in 1815, near the end of the War of 1812, but were defeated by General Andrew Jackson. Half a century later, in 1862, the Union fleet captured the city and held it until the end of the Civil War. After the difficult Reconstruction years, New Orleans once again began to prosper. Today it is one of the country's busiest international ports, serving approximately 100 steamship lines.

The best way to get to know New Orleans is to take a tour or two, via trolley, bus or horse and carriage. The tours cover the highlights of the city and provide a sense of orientation. Information on all of the tours is available, along with maps and brochures, at the New Orleans State and City Tourist Center, 334 Royal Street in the French Quarter.

The French Quarter, or *Vieux Carre*, is actually more Spanish than French in appearance. (*Vieux Carre*, incidentally, means "Old Square.") Bounded by Canal Street, Esplanade, Rampart Street and the Mississippi River, the famous old section was laid out on a gridiron plan in 1721. Much of New Orleans was destroyed by fire in the late 1700s, and the Spanish rulers of the time rebuilt in their own style, creating the arches, balconies and courtyards that are still so typical of the French Quarter.

Jackson Square is the heart of the 13-block-long Vieux Carre. Facing the Square is the Cabildo, a handsome Colonial building that has served as the seat of Louisiana's territorial government for France, Spain, the Confederacy and the United States. Built between 1795 and 1799, the Cabildo replaced an older structure on the same site. The Louisiana Purchase transaction was concluded here in 1803. Today it is a museum containing artifacts of French and Spanish Colonial Louisiana.

The Cathedral of St. Louis King of France also faces Jackson Square. Built in 1794 and remodeled in 1850, it is the oldest active cathedral in the United States. The Presbytere, next to the Cathedral, is almost a twin of the Cabildo. Its construction began in 1791. Among the Presbytere's exhibits are antique toys, vintage Mardi Gras costumes and a portrait gallery. Also adjacent to Jackson Square is the Moon Walk, overlooking the Mississippi.

Some waterfront cities, such as San Francisco and Boston, are built on hills and have sweeping views of the water. But flat New Orleans lies ten feet below the level of the Gulf of Mexico and three to six feet below the Mississippi River's high-water level. The city is surrounded by earthen levees to protect it from floods. Because of this relationship, the river—so important to New Orleans' history—is pretty much invisible except from the levees. One section of levee has always been a promenade; recently it was renamed "The Moon Walk" after former mayor, "Moon" Landrieu, and spruced up with added walkways, steps, benches and fountains. It is a grand place to watch the busy ship traffic on the Mississippi.

Music fans will want to pay a visit to Preservation Hall on St. Peter Street; it is the city's most celebrated jazz club, and old-time musicians still play sets there each night. Jazz was born in New Orleans, as were all the other variations that later evolved—ragtime, swing, the blues and eventually rock. Pete Fountain, Al Hirt and other notables still play traditional jazz in one or another of the city's clubs or hotels.

On Bourbon Street is an odd and eerie little place, the Voodoo Museum. Voodoo and other occult and supernatural items are on display, and Voodoo walking tours of the city start from here every afternoon. One of New Orleans' best-known attractions has long been the Old French Market on Decatur Street. The old vegetable market is still in operation; the other market buildings have been restored and now house an inviting collection of shops, cafes and restaurants.

Restaurants deserve a *special* mention. Many of New Orleans' dining establishments are internationally renowned (and expensive). But you can discover a host of lesser-known restaurants that offer just as good, sometimes even better, food. Practically every cuisine in the world is available, but Creole is king and should be experienced whenever possible. Unique to New Orleans, Creole is a delicious blend of French and Spanish cooking spiced by touches from the West Indies and Africa. No matter what your choice, however, even the simplest of fare is prepared and served with style and elegance. Be sure to come with a healthy appetite. If necessary, go on a diet ahead of time so that you'll be able to indulge yourself in flaky croissants and jam in the mornings, hearty lunches and spectacular dinners. Leave room, too, for the traditional New Orleans' midnight snack of *beignets* and *cafe au lait* at the French Market.

At some point during your stay, go see New Orleans' Garden District, beginning just the other side of Canal Street. It is one of the areas called the "American sections," so named because they were settled by Americans who arrived after the Louisiana Purchase transaction. The residential Garden District is easily reached by bus or the St. Charles trolley (streetcar). Take the latter; you will love it. The legendary streetcar named *Desire* is, sad to say, no longer. *Desire* is now a bus. But the St. Charles streetcar is everything a trolley ought to be; it clangs its leisurely way for six and a half miles from downtown out through the Garden District and on to Carrolton. It travels past grand old Greek Revival mansions built by affluent planters, exquisite gardens and green squares galore, handsome old churches and other structures, and parts of Tulane and Loyola Universities.

River cruises are an excellent way to view New Orleans from a different angle. Take a water cruise back up into the region's swamps and bayous into Cajun country, where the landscape is still much the same as it was when the Acadians arrived from Canada in the 1700s, and where their descendants still live.

If you enjoy crowds and have a taste for unfettered revelry, come to New Orleans for Mardi Gras! One of the most famous celebrations in the world, Mardi Gras is a fabulous extravaganza, a wild and crazy bash in which everyone is invited to participate, masked and costumed, free from any remnant of restraint. *Mardi Gras* means "Fat Tuesday" or Shrove Tuesday, the day before Ash Wednesday, the first day of Lent. The carnival season officially starts on January 6, Twelfth Night, and ends at midnight on Ash Wednesday.

New Orleans has been celebrating Mardi Gras for more than 260 years, ever since the city was founded. In Colonial times the festivities centered mainly around masked balls; the street parades, now scheduled daily, were added later. Dozens of private social organizations called *Krewes* put on today's marvelous costume balls and parades. Unless you know someone in one of the Krewes, however, it is not easy to secure an invitation to a ball. But even so, there is lots of fun to be had just watching the parades or better still, joining in. The entire city goes deliriously insane: the streets are jammed with people; the paraders are outrageously flamboyant; and the music, color and excitement are just too contagious to resist.

Whatever the time of year, there are a large number of guest houses to choose from. They are an old, cherished tradition in New Orleans and include some of the most delightful establishments imaginable. Warning: it is very difficult to find a place to stay during Mardi Gras; so if you intend to be here then, make reservations well in advance, even a year ahead if possible. Also, please inquire about the rates, as many guest houses increase their tariffs during the carnival season, and some raise them for other New Orleans events (Sugar Bowl, Super Bowl, etc.) as well. **75**

GUEST HOUSES

Felton House. A perfect example of a typical French Quarter town house in the Creole style, Felton House has a double front door opening onto a flagstone carriageway that leads to a secluded inner courtyard. The ornate cast-iron balcony over the street is notable for its graceful leaf and grape cluster motif; behind the balcony a handsome second-floor doorway is topped by an arched transom.

Built in 1829-30 by the Soniat-Dufossat family, socially prominent Louisiana plantation owners, the house was purchased by the Felton family in 1945. Over the next few years they worked hard to restore the place, which had fallen into almost total disrepair. In 1980 the house once again changed hands and is now owned and operated by Edwin R. Crossno. But Mrs. Felton, a charming lady in her eighties, has graciously consented to stay on. "Louie," as she is affectionately known, will continue to share with visitors her treasury of stories concerning the house, its ghosts, past owners and unusual guests. The elegant ambiance of Felton House and its tradition of almost four decades of warm hospitality will remain unchanged.

Currently there are five double and four triple rooms for guests, plus one suite of three rooms suitable for four persons, one with three rooms for five persons, and a five-room suite for six persons. Mr. Crossno is planning to restore more rooms in the coming year so as to accommodate a greater number of guests. Each of the air-conditioned rooms has a private bath and is furnished with lovely antiques. There is a fireplace in each room, too; some are wood or coal-burning, others are gas-burning. Maid service is included. The guest quarters all open onto inner balconies above the inviting brick-walled courtyard—a delightfully cool haven of tropical greenery with benches and chairs for relaxing.

In the mornings guests are offered a small breakfast of coffee or tea, freshly squeezed orange juice and croissants, included in the rates. Felton House is ideally located within easy strolling distance of everything in the Vieux Carre, including fine restaurants and shops, the fascinating Old French Market, Jackson Square and the Moon Walk alongside the Mississippi. Off-street parking is available at the house.

Felton House, 1133-35 Chartres Street, New Orleans, LA 70116; (504) 522-0570 or 522-6933. The rates range from $35 to $60 double occupancy with an additional charge of $10 per extra person in room. A one-day deposit is required. MasterCard and Visa accepted, as well as cash, traveler's checks and personal checks (the last with prior approval). Pets *and children are welcome. Open year-around.*

Lafitte Guest House. This lovely old house is located on Bourbon Street in New Orleans' historic French Quarter. It is in the residential section of the quarter, but only a few steps away from all the hustle and bustle of commercial Bourbon Street and the world-renowned antique shops on Royal Street. An elegant French manor house, the building was erected in 1849 as a single family dwelling. It has been meticulously restored and furnished with antiques and reproductions. The present owners, Robert and Claire Guyton, are involved in an on-going refurbishing endeavor, and many of the items of furniture, accessories and oil paintings are from their own personal collection.

The main house, with its several balconies graced by hanging plants, is on a corner overlooking Bourbon and St. Philip Streets. Nine guest rooms are included in the main house, all very large with high ceilings; some have balconies, and others overlook the beautifully landscaped courtyard. In addition, there are five guest rooms in the *garconierre*, or slave quarters. These are smaller but just as charming, and they open out onto the courtyard. All rooms have private baths and are carpeted, air conditioned and heated. Each is individually decorated and offers either queen- or king-size beds.

The tariff includes a Continental breakfast of freshly squeezed orange juice, croissants or brioche and New Orleans-style coffee served in your room, in the splendid parlor or out in the courtyard. All of the attractions in the French Quarter are within walking distance, and it is only a few minutes by car to New Orleans' parks, Lake Pontchartrain and the River Road's great plantation houses. Off-street parking is available; the house is also served by limousine service from the airport directly to the door. The friendly staff will be pleased to help with tours, restaurant reservations or anything else you need to make your stay enjoyable, relaxed and memorable. The Guytons have owned Lafitte House since 1980; they think that it is New Orleans' finest, and they very much want their guests to agree.

Lafitte Guest House, 1003 Bourbon Street, New Orleans, LA 70116; (504) 581-2678. Single $38-$58, double $48-$68, including breakfast. Roll away bed $10; extra person in room $10; extra breakfasts $6. No increased rates for Mardi Gras or the Sugar Bowl games and other events, but please check for minimum number of nights required at these times.

Lafitte Guest House, New Orleans, La.

Visa, MasterCard, American Express, cash and traveler's checks accepted; no personal checks except as advance deposits. No pets, please. Open year-around.

Hotel Maison de Ville. Old World elegance and attentive personal service are the hallmarks of the Maison de Ville. Its staff, beginning with William W. Prentiss, general manager, works hard to assure your every comfort. There is a houseman to take care of cars and a concierge who will book dinner reservations, advise on shopping and arrange sight-seeing tours. Maison de

Ville *is* a guest house, but in many ways it is more in the tradition of the classic small French hotel. It is also expensive.

Amenities, however, are many: beds are turned down each night, and a foil-wrapped chocolate is left on the pillow. Even the nice old custom of shining shoes left outside the bedroom door is still faithfully observed. In the morning, a silver tray bearing freshly squeezed orange juice, croissants, a pot of fragrant New Orleans chicory coffee, a copy of the *Times-Picayune* and a fresh rose is brought to your door or served in the courtyard or salon. Tea, sherry and port are served every afternoon, and coffee, hot chocolate, fruit, sodas, mixers and ice are available throughout the day. All are *lagniappe*—complimentary.

Maison de Ville and its associated Audubon Cottages date back to the late eighteenth century. The main house is actually a group of buildings constructed as a private home; the original slave quarters are thought to be among the oldest structures in New Orleans. All surround a classic New Orleans courtyard with balconies, stairs, wrought-iron furniture, tropical plants and a charming triple-tiered fountain with a fish pond. The formal downstairs salon with marble fireplaces is furnished with exquisite French accent pieces and antique mirrors. The twelve double rooms and two suites available for guests are furnished in such eighteenth- and nineteenth-century antiques as four-posters, marble basins and brass fittings. Some of the accommodations are located in the old slave quarters at the rear of the courtyard. Tennessee Williams, it is said, worked on his play *A Streetcar Named Desire* while staying in room 9. All rooms have private baths.

The seven Audubon Cottages, a block and a half away, also offer accommodations for guests. The cottages, some of which date back to the days of the first Spanish settlers, are clustered around a central courtyard with a swimming pool, behind a 100-year-old stucco wall. They are named for John James Audubon, who resided here with his family in the early 1800s while painting some of his "Birds of America." The original cottages have been renovated into modern living quarters, and several newer ones in the same Creole style have been added. The decor is cool, spare Spanish with brick walls, brick or tile floors and ceilings with exposed beams. Each cottage has at least one bedroom, a private bath, a kitchen kept stocked with soft drinks, lemons and mixers, and its own private courtyard and flower garden. All of the services received by guests in the main house are also provided for cottage guests.

Hotel Maison de Ville, 727 Toulouse Street, New Orleans, LA 70130; (504) 561-5858. Singles from $50; doubles $80-$96; suites $150; cottages from $185. Cash, personal checks and traveler's checks accepted; no credit cards. Valet parking is extra. Pets are allowed only in the cottages. Open year-around.

French Quarter Maisonettes. Mrs. Junius Underwood, Chatelaine . . . that has a nice ring to it, doesn't it? Well, she's a nice lady, and her establishment is one of New Orleans' nicest small guest houses. It is maintained in the best tradition of guest houses—spotlessly spic-and-span, tastefully decorated and run with a delightful personal touch. Guests are treated like members of the family; they are given their own keys, and come and go as they please.

The house, of pale pink stucco, is located in the heart of the French Quarter. It was built in 1825 by the wealthy Soniat-Dufossat family (who also built the Felton House across the street). Another of New Orleans' classic town houses, it boasts graceful balconies outside and in, a flagstoned carriage drive entrance, and a lovely patio where a triple-tiered fountain splashes musically. In the patio you'll probably make friends with Mrs. Underwood's cats; they delight in climbing up and down their very own cat-size circular staircase between the patio and second-floor balcony.

Mrs. Underwood has seven guest rooms, four of which are suites with living room and bedroom. They are all modern in decor. All have private baths and are air conditioned, and most of them open directly onto the patio. No meals are served, but the morning paper is delivered to your door, and guests receive from Mrs. Underwood a personally compiled list of recommended restaurants, bake shops, jazz clubs, tours and various points of interest in New Orleans—practically everything on the list is within an easy walk. Just next door, in fact, is the oldest building in the entire Mississippi Valley, according to record—the Ursuline Convent, begun in 1747. And Beauregard House, where the famed novelist Frances Parkinson Keyes lived (*Dinner at Antoines, The River Road, Crescent Carnival,* etc.) is across the way. Parking is available for a small extra fee, and the house is serviced by the airport limousine.

French Quarter Maisonettes, 1130 Chartres Street, New Orleans, LA 70116; (504) 524-9918. Rates range from $32 to $38, $5 each for extra *person; special rates for Mardi Gras. Cash or traveler's checks accepted. Children over 12 years of age and well-behaved pets are welcome. Open August 1 to the end of June (closed July).*

Maison Ursulines. Jim Weirich and Don Heil are your hosts at Maison Ursulines, another historic old New Orleans house. The property originally formed part of the land granted by the King of France to the Community of the Ursuline Nuns. Their title was formally recorded by the United States in 1824, and a year later the Ursulines sold the property to Joseph Guillot, a prominent New Orleans builder. He erected the house and service quarters; a later owner added to the service building, approximately doubling its size. As in many New Orleans' town houses, there is a carriageway running from the house to a rear wall. But unusual in the French Quarter where land has always been at a premium, the front building is free-standing, with an entrance on each side. There are balconies and a splendid courtyard, of course; the courtyard offers an outstanding collection of trees and flowers, including crape myrtle, magnolias, masses of orchids and azaleas. It is a lovely place to sit and relax; bird feeders and a bird bath attract dozens of birds, too—cardinals, bluejays, mocking birds and many other varieties.

For guests there are five suites, all opening onto the courtyard; each suite accommodates up to three persons. Each contains a sitting room, bedroom, a small kitchenette and private bath. The house is only three blocks from Jackson Square, one block from Royal Street and two from Bourbon Street. Public transportation is available nearby for side trips, and Jim and Don will be delighted to help arrange tours for you, if you like. On-street parking is available. No food is served at Maison Ursulines, but it is within easy walking distance of some of the city's finest restaurants.

Maison Ursulines, 623 Ursulines Street, New Orleans, LA 70116; (504) 529-5489. One or two persons $45, three persons $53. Special rates for Mardi Gras. Cash, personal or traveler's checks accepted; no credit cards. Children over 12 and well-behaved pets are welcome. Open year-around.

LaMothe House. An elegant nineteenth-century mansion, beautifully restored and modernized, LaMothe House is located on tree-shaded Esplanade Avenue in the French Quarter. Mrs. Kenneth A. Langguth serves as hostess and manager, and you'll find her—along with the rest of the staff—warmly welcoming and helpful.

GUEST HOUSES

The three-story house was built around 1800 by Jean LaMothe, a wealthy sugar planter of French descent, originally from the West Indies. LaMothe and his family sought refuge in New Orleans after an insurrection in Santo Domingo. Their new home soon became one of New Orleans' most social, echoing with "the gaiety and gallantry of aristocratic Creole Louisiana."

The house was constructed in the French style as one of the earliest double town houses (for two families) with a *porte cochere*, or carriageway, through the middle. In 1860 the porte cochere became the main hallway leading to twin winding stairways that sweep up to the second-floor reception area and third-floor suites. Much of the original hand-wrought ironwork has been preserved, along with the old cypress floorboards and hand-hewn ceiling timbers. The courtyard still boasts its original flagstones, imported as ships' ballast.

The guest quarters are all furnished with authentic antiques, including canopied beds and huge armoires. There are six rooms with double beds, and six suites. The rooms surround the patio or open onto the balcony above the patio; the suites, except for the Carriage House Suite, are located in the main house just across from the patio. The Gertrude Munson Suite has a double bed and single sofa bed; the Lafayette Suite has twin canopy beds; the Mallard contains a half canopy queen-size bed. The Carriage Room Suite has a king-size bed and double sofa bed and includes a wet bar with refrigerator and ice maker. The remaining suites each contain three beds, two doubles and one twin. All accommodations are air conditioned, have private baths, room telephones, color television and free in-room coffee. Daily laundry and dry cleaning service is available except on weekends.

Complimentary *petit dejeuner* is served every morning in the handsomely appointed dining room; guests are offered a choice of fruit juices, warm sweet rolls, coffee, Sanka or tea. The coffee is served from a 200-year-old Sheffield urn. As for anything else you may desire while staying at LaMothe House, just ask. Guided bus or limousine tours and bayou tours can be arranged with pick-up at the door. Free parking is provided; there is also airport limousine service. French Quarter minibuses stop at the corner every few minutes, but the house is within walking distance of just about every place of interest in the quarter.
LaMothe House, 621 Esplanade Avenue, New Orleans, LA 70116; (504)

947-1161 or 947-1162. *(In July and August call 947-1469.) One double bed $43; twin beds $45; suites $56 and $60; $10 extra per person in suites. Rates are higher for Christmas, Thanksgiving, Easter, Mardi Gras and Sugar Bowl. Visa, MasterCard and American Express accepted; personal checks accepted for deposits only. No pets allowed. Open from September 1 to end of June (closed in July and August).*

The Cornstalk Hotel. Legend has it that *Uncle Tom's Cabin* was written at The Cornstalk Hotel; true or not, this attractive French Quarter guest house is just as famous for its ornate cast-iron fence with a very realistic cornstalk motif. The two-story, balconied white house, owned by Mrs. Rose Noble, is about 200 years old. Each of the fourteen comfortable guest rooms is individually decorated and has a private bath. The entire house is furnished with a splendid collection of antiques; ask your hostess to tell you about some of her favorites.

Mrs. Noble offers a complimentary Continental breakfast of coffee or tea, orange juice and sweet rolls served in the courtyard, on the front balcony or brought to your room. She will also be happy to direct you to some of the city's fine restaurants

Cornstalk Hotel, New Orleans, La.

for other meals. Limited parking is available at the house.

The Cornstalk Hotel, 915 Royal Street, New Orleans, LA 70116; (504) 523-1515. Singles $40; doubles $45-$65, depending on the size and location of the room. Extra person in room $5. The rates change for Mardi Gras, Sugar Bowl and Super Bowl events. Visa, MasterCard and American express cards accepted. No pets, please. Open year-around.

Hansel & Gretle Guest House. Larry Jones and Ernie Robichaux are the proprietors of the Hansel & Gretle House, a cluster of thirteen post-Civil War Creole cottages in New Orleans' French Quarter. Your hosts describe the place as "unpretentious and comfortable."

Thirty-seven rooms in a variety of styles are available for guests. All the rooms are air conditioned and have private baths, color television and daily maid service. The cottages look out onto courtyards adorned with tropical plants and Spanish moss, and there is a small swimming pool. A Continental breakfast included in the rates is served in the pleasant breakfast room. Free parking is available and guided tours pick up at the front door.

Hansel & Gretle Guest House, 916 Burgundy Street, New Orleans, LA 70116; (504) 524-0141. (Phone between 10 A.M. and 5 P.M. Monday through Friday.) Also phone toll free 1 (800) 535-7785. Rates range from $32.50 to $49.50 and up, depending on single, double or king-size bed preference and individual room. These rates do not apply during Mardi Gras, Super Bowl, Sugar Bowl or other special events. Cash or traveler's checks accepted; American Express accepted with a $100 limit. No pets, please. Open year-around except for three weeks after Thanksgiving.

ParkView Guest House. Located in the lovely Garden District, ParkView claims to be New Orleans' first guest house. The handsome Victorian mansion was built for the New Orleans' Cotton Exchange Exposition held in Audubon Park in the 1880s. The house overlooks Audubon Park and is across the street from Loyola, Tulane, Newcomb and Dominican colleges on St. Charles Avenue.

Robert Hudson and Zafer B. Zaitoon operate the recently restored ParkView. Of their 25 guest rooms, 13 have one double bed, and 12 have two double beds. All are air conditioned and attractively furnished with period pieces and some antiques. Ten rooms have private baths; the other rooms share six baths. Monday through Friday guests are invited to enjoy a complimentary Continental breakfast, served from 7:30 to 9:00

A.M.: coffee, orange juice, croissants, butter and jelly. Free on-street parking is available; and the ParkView is on the St. Charles streetcar line, 15 minutes from the French Quarter and downtown New Orleans. The beautiful homes of the Garden District are all around, and Audubon Park with its newly remodeled zoo is just across the way.

ParkView Guest House, 7004 St. Charles Avenue, New Orleans, LA 70118; (504) 866-5580. Rates: $23-$35 per night; $138-$210 per week single occupancy, depending on the room. Extra person $6 daily, $36 weekly. Monthly rates are also available. During New Orleans' special events (except Mardi Gras), add $10 on room, $16 for daily double occupancy. Please inquire for rates during Mardi Gras. Cash or traveler's checks accepted. Preferably no children; definitely no pets. Open year-around.

The Columns. Most of New Orleans' Garden District mansions may only be looked at; this stately manor house also welcomes guests for overnight or longer. Appropriately named for its large, white Southern Colonial columns, the impressive Victorian Italianate structure was designed in 1883 by Thomas Sully, a nationally prominent New Orleans architect. Today it is owned by Claire and Jacques Creppel, who thoroughly enjoy

The Columns Hotel, New Orleans, La.

GUEST HOUSES

pointing out some of the house's architectural treasures to their guests. Especially noteworthy is the original winding stairway with hand-turned mahogany railings. Many of the furnishings are also the originals, as are the moldings, cornices and the beautiful stained glass skylight at the top of the stairs.

The Columns is a large house; its 30 guest rooms are spacious and airy and have comfortable beds and period furniture; some of the rooms have balconies. Twelve have private baths; the remainder share five baths. All accommodations are air conditioned and heated. Broad porches and green lawns outside offer shady, relaxing places to sit and are ideal for children. If you wish, the Creppels will arrange for a baby-sitter.

Morning coffee is included in the rates, and a delicious Southern breakfast is available, served in the dining room for a modest extra price. Lunches, also, may be requested. A garage across the street provides parking for a low fee; restaurants and shops are within walking distance and the St. Charles streetcar transports passengers directly to downtown New Orleans and the French Quarter.

The Columns, 3811 St. Charles Avenue, New Orleans, LA 70114; (504) 899-9308. Single with shared bath $30; double with shared bath $40; double with private bath $50-$60. Mardi Gras season rates are double. All major credit cards, cash and traveler's checks are accepted. No pets, please; children are welcome. Open year-around.

Mississippi

Creamy blossoms in the spring, pretty girls in hoopskirts welcoming visitors to white-columned antebellum mansions, cotton fields and Civil War battlegrounds—Mississippi offers them all, in abundance. Called The Magnolia State, Mississippi is just as romantically Deep South as its nickname implies. But it is far from being a living monument to the past. Modern industry thrives in Mississippi, as does agriculture. Today, however, soybeans have supplanted cotton as the major cash crop.

Much of the state's early history is shared with that of neighboring Louisiana. Hernando de Soto explored the region in the mid-1500s, discovering the Mississippi River. Robert Cavelier, Sieur de La Salle, claimed the entire river valley for France in 1682 and named it *Louisiana* in honor of Louis XIV. In 1699, Pierre Lemoyne, Sieur de Iberville, brought a band of colonists from France and founded Biloxi. Lemoyne's brother, Jean Baptiste, established Mississippi's second French settlement at Fort Rosalie (later Natchez) in 1716; two years later he founded New Orleans.

France ceded its territory east of the Mississippi River, except for New Orleans, to England in 1763. The upper Mississippi region became part of the Georgia colony, the lower area part of British West Florida. During the American Revolution, while the British were busy trying to hang on to their northern colonies, the Spanish seized West Florida. In 1798, after the Revolution, the newly formed United States government created the Mississippi Territory, which included part of present-day Mississippi and Alabama. The territory was later extended north to the Tennessee border and, after settlers took part of West Florida away from Spain in 1810, it was extended south to the Gulf of Mexico. In 1817 the Mississippi Territory was divided: Alabama became a separate territory, and Mississippi joined the Union as its twentieth state.

Mississippi prospered in the years before the Civil War. Great cotton plantations brought enormous wealth to their owners;

most of the state's majestic mansions were built during that era. Mississippi seceded from the Union on January 9, 1861; during the Civil War years the state was the scene of many fierce battles and skirmishes. It was readmitted to the Union in 1870, but some twenty years passed before Mississippi really began to recover from the disastrous effects of the war and its immediate aftermath.

Today, Mississippi is again serene and thriving. It is a beautiful state: the land ranges from rolling hills and large tracts of green forest to the flat, rich soil of the Delta and a coastline of white sand beaches. It offers travelers a host of historical sites, numerous coastal resort areas and excellent hunting and fishing.

BILOXI

Biloxi, the oldest town in the Mississippi Valley, is situated on the Gulf of Mexico. It was the first capital of the Louisiana Territory, which stretched from the gulf all the way to Canada. When Pierre Lemoyne settled there at the end of the seventeenth century, it was still inhabited by the Biloxi Indians, members of the Sioux tribe. *Biloxi* is an Indian word meaning "First People."

A charming old town, Biloxi has been a popular year-around resort since the mid-1800s. Its warm semi-tropical climate causes camellias, roses and magnolias to bloom even in winter. Biloxi is renowned for its superb fishing, a magnificent 26-mile-long beach and the colorful annual Blessing of the Shrimp Fleet. The Shrimp Festival is usually held in early June and includes street dances (called *fais do do*) and a parade of hundreds of festively decorated boats.

Deer Island, half a mile offshore, was once a stopping place for pirates. Legend claims that some of their ill-gotten treasure was buried here. Ship Island, twelve miles out, offers excellent surf fishing and swimming. The British used the island as a base for their fleet when they attacked New Orleans in 1815. During summer months visitors may tour an old fort on the island. Partly constructed just before the Civil War, the fort was occupied both by Confederate and Federal soldiers. It was called Fort Twiggs by the Southern forces and was renamed Fort Massachusetts by the Federal troops who captured it in 1861.

Among Biloxi's many other historic sites is *Beauvoir*, last home of Confederate President Jefferson Davis. The house, gardens and grounds have been carefully restored, and original Davis family furniture and personal possessions are on view.

Also on the grounds are a Confederate Museum, housed in an old hospital building constructed for Civil War veterans, and the Library Pavilion, which contains Davis' desk and books.

THE NATCHEZ TRACE

One of Mississippi's greatest attractions is the historic Natchez Trace, once an ancient Indian wilderness trail. Indian mounds, village sites and shell heaps along the Trace indicate that it was regularly used as early as 8000 years ago. When white people came, they too followed the old trail; by the early 1800s the Natchez Trace had become the most heavily traveled road in the Old Southwest. Settlers seeking homesteads traversed its length; post riders carried the mail along the trail; General Andrew Jackson and his soldiers walked it to and from the Battle of New Orleans. Goods were floated down the Mississippi on flatboats to Natchez or New Orleans; the return journey was made overland via the Natchez Trace. Outlaws, too, used the trail to prey on innocent travelers.

Now, the Natchez Trace is a scenic parkway maintained by the National Park Service. A few sections are not yet completed, but when they are the road will extend for 447 miles running diagonally across Mississippi northeast from Natchez, through a portion of Alabama and then into southern Tennessee and up to Nashville. Historic markers along the way tell the romantic story of the Trace, indicating remnants of the original trail and pointing to various exhibits and nearby places of interest.

Jackson, Mississippi's capital, is just a short distance from the Trace. Named for Andrew Jackson, it sits atop high bluffs overlooking the Pearl River. During the Civil War, most of the city was burned by General Sherman's troops. Jackson is home of the Mississippi State Fair each October; it is also famed for the Spring Pilgrimage during which many of its lovely old houses and gardens are open to the public. The Mississippi State Historical Society has many fascinating exhibits; the society is located in the Old Capitol Building. The handsome Greek Revival structure was begun in 1833 and was completely restored in the late 1950s.

Another scene of Civil War strife, Vicksburg is not far from the Natchez Trace Parkway, northwest of Jackson. In June 1862 Vicksburg was held by the Confederates. Its batteries, situated on bluffs above the Mississippi River, were in excellent position to fire upon Northern forces trying to move up or down the river.

General Ulysses S. Grant was determined to take the town; after several attempts to storm it failed, he decided to surround the place and starve it into submission. The siege lasted for 47 days. Vicksburg's inhabitants dug caves in which to hide from the almost constant barrage of cannon and mortar fire. But the lack of incoming supplies took its toll, and starvation became a reality. The Confederate forces surrendered the town on July 4. Although the war continued for two more years, historians feel that the Southern cause was lost forever at Vicksburg.

The Vicksburg National Military Park and Cemetery runs along the edge of the city and is open daily for touring. At the Old Court House Museum in town you can wander through a series of rooms displaying Civil War, pioneer and Indian artifacts and other items.

For a change of pace from Civil War history, try the Emerald Mound, on the Parkway twelve miles northeast of Natchez. The third largest Indian mound in the United States, it extends over eight acres. The unknown Indians who built it (about 600 years ago) designed the mound as a flat temple base, not for burial purposes as was the custom among earlier tribes.

NATCHEZ

Natchez, at the southwestern end of the Natchez Trace, is probably Mississippi's most visited town, and it is one of the oldest in the state. The Natchez Indians, for whom the town is named, hunted buffalo and worshipped sun gods here for generations before the first European came. The French explorer La Salle saw the bluffs of Natchez when he was roaming about the region in 1682 and realized that whoever controlled those heights would also control the river. Fort Rosalie was built on the site in 1716.

The Natchez Indians accepted the newcomers peaceably enough until 1729, when they massacred the entire French garrison. The French quickly took revenge and chased the Indians out of the region. After the end of the French and Indian Wars, Natchez came under British control, which lasted until the American Revolution when it was seized by the Spanish. Finally, in 1798 the United States took over Natchez as part of the Mississippi Territory.

Today Natchez prides itself on being "a museum of the Old South" with an unmatched collection of nearly 100 spectacular antebellum mansions and plantation houses. They have such beguiling names as Airlie, Mistletoe, Mount Repose, Green

Leaves and Ravenna, and each has a story. During Natchez' annual Spring and Fall Pilgrimages, thirty of these homes are open to the public for daily tours and nighttime candlelight viewings. The town also puts on a full-dress Confederate Pageant depicting scenes from plantation life; the pageant is presented at the City Auditorium four nights a week during Pilgrimage season. (The Spring Pilgrimage is held late March to early April; Fall Pilgrimage is usually in early to middle October.)

But if you cannot come to Natchez for Pilgrimage, you will still find a great many attractions available throughout the rest of the year. Fourteen antebellum homes are open year-around; ask for information about The Tour of Historic Homes and Gardens at the Chamber of Commerce, 300 N. Commerce Street. There, too, you can pick up a walking-tour map of the town.

One stop not to be missed is Connelly's Tavern (circa 1795) on Ellicott's Hill above the Mississippi. It is an authentically restored old tavern with a colorful history. And there is Natchez-Under-the-Hill, which once was a notorious, rowdy settlement at the base of the city's bluffs, much favored by river travelers as a place to drink, gamble, find a less-than-ladylike woman and most likely have an enjoyable fight or two. Over the years, the disreputable old hell-hole became virtually a ghost town, but it has recently been partially restored—not, however, in the raunchy style of its heyday! Natchez-Under-the-Hill now offers restaurants and lounges that only *reflect* the area's bad old days.

Another interesting place to visit is the Grand Village of the Natchez Indians, which presents a museum, nature trails, archaeological sites and a slide presentation telling about the sun-worshipping Natchez people.

At Jefferson College (no longer a school), three miles east of town, you may explore the old church were Aaron Burr was arraigned for treason in 1807. And Spring Plantation, where Andrew Jackson is said to have been married, is located 20 miles northeast of Natchez on U.S. 61 in Fayette. Built between 1786 and 1790, the house contains the original mantelpieces and woodwork, along with displays of Civil War and railroad memorabilia.

Natchez also offers two outstanding guest houses: The Burn and Monmouth. Both are historic, antique-filled mansions with lengthy histories and offer luxurious accommodations for

travelers. Also, all those splendid old plantations in Louisiana's
St. Francisville area over on the other side of the Mississippi
River are within easy driving distance.

The Burn. Mr. and Mrs. Reuben Lee Harper, Jr., (better known
as Buzz and Bobbie), are your hosts in their lovely old Natchez
home, The Burn. Back in the nineteenth century, a young man
named John P. Walworth was traveling down the Mississippi by
steamboat on his way to New Orleans to seek his fortune. He
came ashore at Natchez, and the town appealed to him so
much he decided to stay. Walworth built The Burn around 1832
and named it for a small brook ("burn" in Scottish) that once
passed through the property.

During the Civil War, The Burn was occupied by Union
troops, who used it as their headquarters and then made it a
Federal hospital. Buzz and Bobbie Harper bought the property
in 1978. Before that they were the proprietors of another Natchez treasure, a 1790 mansion and guest house called The
Wigwam, so called because it was built atop an old Indian
mound. The Wigwam has since been sold to new owners and
no longer takes guests.

The Burn, however, offers six delightful rooms for visitors; all
are furnished in exquisite antiques. Located in the old slave
quarters, each of the rooms accommodates two or more persons; each is air conditioned and has its own private bath and
television.

The main house has four white columns and a broad piazza;
brick steps lead up to the wide front door. Comfortable chairs
on the porch provide a cool place to sit and look out over the
gently sloping lawns, tall shade trees and masses of green shrubbery and flowers. The Burn is noted for its gardens, including a
charming herb garden with a marvelous old fountain. There is
also a swimming pool for guest use.

Buzz and Bobbie serve their guests a complimentary
Southern plantation-style breakfast in the dining room. In the
afternoon, refreshments are offered in the elegant downstairs
parlor. Guests are given a tour of the house, during which they
see the magnificent semi-spiral stairway and the Harpers'
superb collection of antique furnishings, porcelain and crystal.

Parking is available on the grounds, and there are restaurants
and shops within easy walking distance of the house. The
Mississippi River and Natchez-Under-the-Hill are also close by.

The Harpers will be delighted to suggest some good places to eat; in addition, they are always happy to share their knowledge of Natchez history.

The Burn, 712 North Union Street, Natchez, MI 39120; (601) 445-8566 or 442-1344. Single $55, double $60, extra person in room $15. Personal checks or cash accepted. No children under school age, please. Open year-around.

The Burn, Natchez, Mississippi

Monmouth. One of Mississippi's most historic homes, Monmouth is an imposing Greek Revival structure set atop a hill and surrounded by 26 acres of beautifully landscaped grounds. The two-story brick mansion is fronted by a broad white portico with four massive square columns.

John Hankinson, a Natchez postmaster originally from Monmouth, New Jersey, built the house around 1818. Shortly thereafter, yellow fever broke out in Natchez-Under-the-Hill, and the Hankinsons were asked to nurse a man who had contracted the disease. They caught the fever and died within a week. Monmouth was sold in 1825 at a public auction for

Monmouth, Natchez, Mississippi.

$10,000. Then in 1826 John Anthony Quitman purchased the property for his bride, Eliza.

Quitman had come to Natchez in 1821, penniless but with a law degree. He joined a local legal firm; later he served as a major general in the Mexican-American War. Quitman and his Mississippi troops proved themselves heroes in the war and returned to wild acclaim. The U.S. Congress honored him for his bravery with a golden sword, presented by President James K. Polk. The sword, which had disappeared for a number of years, was eventually rediscovered and is now displayed at Monmouth.

In later years, Quitman was named chancellor of Mississippi, then served as congressman, and finally governor. His career seemed to have no bounds. Then at a banquet in Washington given by President James Buchanan, General Quitman was poisoned. Since it is reported that he possessed an extremely charismatic personality and was beloved by all, it would seem that the poisoning must have been accidental. In any case, he managed to return to Natchez, where he died some time later.

His funeral was one of the grandest ever seen in Mississippi:

church bells tolled, flags flew at half mast and all business was suspended. A Mississippi author of that day wrote: "John A. Quitman was the most popular man in all America."

Another of Monmouth's noted owners was Mrs. Ann Gwin Barham, one of the founders of the Natchez Pilgrimage. In 1978, Mr. and Mrs. Ronald Riches bought the place from her heirs. Ron and Lani Riches came to Natchez from Los Angeles. They stopped here while on a trip East and fell in love with the historic Mississippi River town. Deciding that they would like to purchase one of its fine old houses, they inquired about them and discovered that Monmouth was available.

Although sadly deteriorated, the building was structurally sound, and so the Riches proceeded to meticulously restore the place. Today the house and its grounds, listed in the National Register of Historic Places, once again appear as they did when General Quitman was in residence. In August 1980, Ron and Lani opened part of Monmouth for guests.

There are seven elegantly furnished guest rooms located in the completely renovated old slave quarters. The rooms all have modern, private baths and are done in antiques carefully chosen by Lani Riches, who is a professional decorator. Each of the rooms accommodates two or more persons. Guests are offered a complimentary Continental breakfast, served on a silver tray in their room or in the old slave kitchen.

The plantation has beautiful gardens and wooded areas, and there are numerous pathways and nature trails for rambling. There is a tiny, historic cemetery on the property, too. Parking is available, and you can walk to many of Natchez' restaurants, shops and the like; they are only about half a mile away.

Monmouth, 36 Melrose Avenue, Natchez, MI 39120; (601) 442-5852. (Corner of State and Melrose.) Single $55, double $60, extra person in room $15. Visa, MasterCard, or personal checks accepted. No pets, please, and no children under 14 years. Open year-around.

North Carolina

New Englanders, on the whole, tend to believe that their six-state region is the most beautiful, varied and historic in the East (if not the entire country). North Carolinians, however, know very well that *their* state—all by itself—offers tough competition. Its citizens could brag and say that North Carolina is even better. But they are not that immodest; instead, they let the state speak for itself.

North Carolina's mountains include many peaks higher than those in New England. Mt. Mitchell is in fact the highest point east of the Mississippi. Through these magnificent mountains runs one of the country's most spectacular roads, the Blue Ridge Parkway. The state's seacoast, though not as dramatically rock bound as New England's, offers an abundance of broad, sandy beaches. Offshore, a chain of barrier reefs, sand dunes and narrow islands curves along the coast for hundreds of miles. Every inch of the coast is saturated with history—the tale of a lost colony, reams of romantic pirate lore, sinister legends of ships lured to their doom and the site of the Wright Brothers' first flight.

Even in the matter of chronological firsts, North Carolina comes off a winner: the state's earliest English colony predated the Pilgrims' landing in Massachusetts by 35 years. As for weather, North Carolina boasts a delightfully benign climate all year around. Yet (making matters worse) some of the best winter skiing in the East may be enjoyed nowadays on North Carolina's slopes! It's all enough to make a native New Englander choke on his or her baked beans and brown bread.

North Carolina's intriguing story begins with an unsolved mystery. In 1584 Sir Walter Raleigh sent English explorers to investigate the southeastern coast of North America. They reported favorably on the region, and a colonizing mission was dispatched the following year. That first colony was established on Roanoke Island, in what is now North Carolina. It was abandoned a year later, but in 1587 a second group of colonists arrived, led by John White. His granddaughter, Virginia Dare, was the first child of English parents to be born in America.

White sailed back to England for supplies, but because of problems with the Spanish Armada, he and his shipload of goods were unable to set sail again for America until 1590. Upon arrival, White discovered to his dismay that the entire colony—every last soul—had vanished. All that was left was a fort-like enclosure and the word *Croatan* (the name of a friendly local Indian tribe) carved on a post. Because there was no evidence of a violent attack or fire, White was forced to believe that the colonists had all gone off to join the Indians. The puzzle remains to this day; although many differing theories have been put forth, no actual trace of those lost colonists has ever been found.

One might think that the terrors and hardships of the New World would have caused England to give up the idea of colonizing the land. But tales of its riches continued to spark the acquisitive interest of the crown, and in 1607 the first permanent English colony in America was settled in Jamestown, Virginia. In 1663 Charles II granted the territory south of Virginia to eight Lords Proprietors, who named it *Carolina* after the king. The huge tract was divided into North and South Carolina in 1710; 18 years later the proprietors sold their rights back to the crown and the Carolinas became royal colonies, each ruled by a royal governor appointed by the king—until the American Revolution.

The citizens of both Carolinas were, from the start, a free-thinking lot. Most were emigrants from England, Scotland, Ireland and Germany who crossed the Atlantic in search of a new life and who scorned repression of any kind. All hardy individualists, they made the proprietary and royal colony years turbulent ones for their rulers. In April 1776 North Carolina was the first colony to vote for independence. Although the British tried to retain their hold over the feisty excolonists, they were forced out for good after losing several battles. Following the Revolution, the state refused to ratify the newly created Constitution until the Bill of Rights was adopted.

North Carolina once again showed its independent nature at the start of the Civil War in 1861 by being the last state to secede from the Union. Once involved, however, it fought hard. Some 40,000 North Carolinians lost their lives in the war, more than any other Confederate state.

Geographically, North Carolina has three distinct regions: the coastal plain and offshore islands, the Piedmont or midlands, and the mountains. Each region contains a multitude of places to see and things to do for the vacationer. Those whose tastes run to history seek out battlegrounds, exciting historical drama and charming old towns with fascinating pasts. For scenery buffs, the state offers a remarkably diverse choice of attractions: ocean beaches; winding mountain roads with breathtaking vistas at every turn; hillsides blooming with rhododendron and mountain laurel in the spring and flaming with startling color in the fall; freshwater lakes, great rivers, tumbling streams and vast green forests.

Collectors of native crafts will find a wealth of unique handmade items, and for the sports-minded there are swimming, boating, fishing and hunting, hiking and horseback riding, skiing and superb golf. The North Carolinians themselves are unpretentiously friendly and very hospitable, with a wickedly dry sense of humor. Stay awhile at one of the many guest houses scattered throughout the state. It is the best way to really get to know the region and its people.

COASTAL REGION/THE OUTER BANKS

A visit to North Carolina should definitely include a drive along the Outer Banks, part of the chain of long, narrow islands and sandy reefs that stretches in a 325-mile curve along the coastline. It is possible to explore the Outer Banks briefly by just driving through (about a 90-mile trip), but they really deserve a lengthier stay. The large assortment of overnight accommodations for travelers includes several guest houses.

Before beginning the tour of the Outer Banks, take a side trip to historic Edenton, on Albemarle Sound. (From Elizabeth City take U.S. 17 southwest.) Edenton has been called North Carolina's prettiest town. Once a prosperous seaport, now it is a dreamy old community filled with flowers, trees and lovely eighteenth- and nineteenth-century homes. In spring masses of jonquils, roses, irises, lilies and tulips bloom everywhere. The narrow streets are shaded by huge old elms, magnolias and pecans. You can explore best on foot—just follow the Historic Edenton Walking Tour. Stop at the Barker House Visitor Center for information, or for a personally guided tour. Be sure to walk along King Street to see its fine collection of Georgian, Federal and Greek Revival homes.

Settlers came to the area as early as 1658. Edenton was incorporated in 1722 and became the first capital of the province of North Carolina. Several noted Revolutionary patriots lived here, and during the Revolution local exporters defied British blockades by sending desperately needed supplies to Washington's army. In 1774 the ladies of Edenton staged their own Tea Party. In the earliest known instance of political action by American women, 51 of them signed a resolution supporting the acts of the rebellious provincial congress. They declared that until the hated British taxes were abolished they would drink no more tea, nor would they wear English clothing.

To get to the Outer Banks from Edenton, retrace your route back to Elizabeth City and then take U.S. 158 east and south. Or follow N.C. 32 and 37 down to U.S. 64, which will take you east to Roanoke Island and the Fort Raleigh Historic Site. The area in which the lost English colony was located has been ex-cavated, and the fort has been reconstructed to appear as it was when the colonists built it. A Pulitzer Prize winning historical drama, *The Lost Colony*, graphically and movingly portrays the incredibly hard life those early settlers had to endure. Per-formed nightly except Sundays from late June through August, the production (the country's first outdoor dramma) has been running since 1937.

While you are in the vicinity, be sure to see the Elizabethan Gardens not far from the Fort. They include the Great Lawn, Sunken Garden, the Queen's Rose Garden, gardens of wild flowers and herbs and a fine collection of ancient garden statuary.

From Roanoke Island it is a short drive east and north to Kill Devil Hills, just south of Kitty Hawk. Here you can visit the Wright Brothers National Memorial, the actual site of the famed brothers' first powered airplane flight in 1903. There is a full-scale reproduction of the original plane, among other in-teresting exhibits.

Now go south, to the resort area of Nags Head. Nags Head is said to be named for a villainous method of wrecking ships prac-ticed long ago (according to legend) by some of the local in-habitants. They would wait for a dark, moonless night, then hang lanterns from the necks of horses and walk them along the dunes. Ships making their way along the coast would be lured by the misleading lights onto the dangerous shoals and wrecked; their cargoes were "salvaged" by the wily thieves.

The Cape Hatteras National Seashore begins at Whalebone Junction, a short distance south of Nags Head. A hard-surface

road (N.C. 12) runs for 70 miles along the seashore; Hatteras Inlet is crossed via a free auto ferry. The Seashore is a shifting,
always changing world of sand dunes, sea, wind, marshes, beach
grasses, birds and the skeletons of wrecked sailing ships. There
are designated parking areas for cars. Visitors are advised not to
drive onto the sand because it is very soft, and getting stuck
(which can happen only too easily) is a real aggravation. Also be
cautious about swimming, especially if the surf is running.
There are dangerous currents and rip tides, particularly near inlets. The National Park Service people recommend swimming
only at beaches where lifeguards are on duty.

Bird-watchers delight in the Bodie Island Marshes, near the
north entrance to the National Seashore. From various parking
areas you may see egrets, herons, glossy ibises and many other
species. A bit further along are the stark bones of the *Laura
Barnes*, wrecked in 1921. Keep your eyes open for the remains
of other wrecked ships, too; more than 600 have been recorded.
Next you will come to Pea Island Wildlife Refuge where snow
geese by the thousands come to spend the winter months. And
way down at the bottom of Hatteras Island is the Cape Hatteras
Lighthouse, standing since 1870, the tallest lighthouse on the
North American coast. It is open to the public; the 198-feet-
high structure with 268 steps is worth climbing for a fantastic
view.

Ocracoke, on Ocracoke Island where the National Seashore
comes to an end, is a picturesque fishing community much like
a New England coastal village. The ship carrying Sir Walter
Raleigh's 1585 colony ran aground here on its way to Roanoke
Island, and its passengers were forced to go ashore while repairs
were made. In the 1700s, settlers from the mainland used the
island for grazing livestock. And lots of pirates—including the
infamous Edward Teach, known as Blackbeard—used
Ocracoke Inlet as a refuge from government ships and as a base
for their nefarious operations.

There are as many fables told about Teach and his buccaneer-
ing career as there were hairs in his bushy black beard, and most
of the stories include at least an element of truth. Pirates were
supposed to be fierce, but Blackbeard apparently made
fierceness almost an art. It is said that he had a habit of braiding
his beard and tying the braids with ribbon. A more colorful tale
claims that he braided pieces of hemp soaked in lime water or
tallow into his beard. Before charging into battle, he would set
the hemp afire. Prospective victims would understandably

quail before the awful sight of the notorious pirate coming at them like Satan himself, wisps of smoke curling up around his fearsome visage. Still another report says that he would stick long, lighted matches under his hat to create the same effect.

In any case, Blackbeard was obviously a formidable and imaginative foe. He backed up his early version of psychological warfare by arming himself with several daggers, a cutlass and at least six pistols primed, cocked and ready to shoot. His vessel was a captured French merchantman, which he converted into a 40-gun marauder called *Queen Anne's Revenge.*

Blackbeard terrorized the sea-lanes from Virginia to the Caribbean for about two years, from 1716 to 1718. At one point he made an agreement with North Carolina's royal governor, Charles Eden: in return for protection, the pirate would share his ill-gotten prizes. Making Ocracoke Inlet his base, Blackbeard continued to plunder ships at sea and also began to harass landowners along the North Carolina coastline. When not so engaged, he shared a happy home life with his fourteenth wife in the small town of Bath.

The coastal planters soon became fed up with Blackbeard's depredations. Since they could not trust their own governor, they petitioned Alexander Spotswood, lieutenant governor of Virginia, for help. Spotswood dispatched two British sloops under the command of Lieutenant Robert Maynard. On November 21, 1718, the Naval vessels caught up with Blackbeard in Ocracoke Inlet and engaged him in a bloody battle. Maynard succeeded in killing the pirate in a hand-to-hand struggle.

Blackbeard's head was then removed and attached to the end of Maynard's bowsprit; the victorious ship sailed back along the coast to Virginia, triumphantly displaying the horrid token to prove that Blackbeard's reign of terror had truly ended. As with all pirate stories, Blackbeard's includes tempting legends of treasure buried along the Atlantic coast; but nothing has ever been found, and the likelihood is that the old villain spent it all.

To reach the southern coast of North Carolina, take the toll ferry from Ocracoke over to Cedar Island, a two and a half hour trip. Advance reservations are necessary. From Cedar Island, take U.S. 70 to Morehead City; then follow the coast south to Wilmington and miles of marvelous beaches.

Before heading south, though, take a short jaunt northwest of Morehead City (on U.S. 70) to New Bern, North Carolina's first permanent Colonial capital. Settled by Germans and Swiss

Blackbeard's Lodge, Ocracoke, N.C.

seeking religious and political freedom in the New World, New Bern was named for the city in Switzerland. One of the country's most elegant houses, the Tryon Palace, is open to visitors (except on Mondays). The mansion was built in the late 1760s for the Royal Governor, William Tryon, and later became the first state capitol building. In 1798 the house, except for one wing, was destroyed by fire. For 154 years it lay in ruins; but in 1952 restoration was begun, and today the Tryon Palace is an authentic and very beautiful example of the finest in eighteenth-century architecture. Its furnishings and lovely English gardens are equally as authentic. Costumed hostesses guide you through the house; the gardens may be toured on your own.

Wilmington is another historic town, now grown into a city. Walking or motor tours will lead you to several fine old mansions, including the 1771 Burgwin-Wright House (now a museum) where the English General Cornwallis had his headquarters. Wilmington's old Cotton Exchange building has been restored to house a number of specialty shops and restaurants. Children will enjoy a visit to the U.S.S. *North Carolina* Battleship Memorial, and history buffs of all ages should make a point of visiting the Blockade Runner Museum (15 miles south of the city).

Wilmington was one of the major Confederate ports; during the Civil War more than 2000 ships managed to evade the Northern blockade and deliver goods here to be dispersed to the rest of the struggling South. The Museum tells the story with fascinating dioramas and displays, including a 40-foot scale model of Fort Fisher. There is a gripping sight and sound dramatization of the massive fort's efforts to protect the blockade runners as they carried out their dangerous mission under the noses of Union gunboats.

Orton Plantation, 18 miles south of Wilmington overlooking Cape Fear River, offers a year-around display of beautifully landscaped gardens set amidst broad avenues of live oaks. Part of the magnificent antebellum mansion with its graceful white columns dates back to 1730; it is not open to the public. Airlie Gardens, east of Wilmington, are also situated on the grounds of a great long-ago plantation. Airlie is especially lovely in the spring when the azaleas are in bloom.

L. V. Gaskill/Guests. L. (for Lloyd) V. Gaskill is unique. He is 91 years old and still welcomes guests to his unpretentious country home. But only when he is up to it; so be *sure* to call in advance for reservations. He began, he explains, "just by being hospitable to folks who were unable to get a room anywhere else." Since then, he has had guests from all over the world, and they have included "everyone from bank presidents to ditch diggers."

Mr. Gaskill's 70-year-old white frame house has a wide front porch. It is located in the center of Roanoke Island, ten minutes from the ocean. The house's accommodations include two double and two triple rooms and two shared bathrooms. You will need a car for exploring and for reaching restaurants, shops, etc. Mr. Gaskill does not offer meals.

L. V. Gaskill/Guests, Wanchese, NC 27981; (919) 473-2905. Rates: $15 per couple; $20 for three or more. Cash only. No pets, please. Dates open: whenever Mr. Gaskill says you can come.

Ye Olde Cherokee Inn. A rambling three-story structure with broad porches, Ye Olde Cherokee is right across the road from the Atlantic Ocean, within sight of the Wright Brothers National Memorial in Kill Devil Hills. Built in the 1940s, the building was once a hunting and fishing lodge; then it became a boarding house renowned for its family-style meals, especially the country ham and biscuit breakfasts.

Nowadays, Bob and Phyl Combs operate the Olde Cherokee as a guest house and offer a heap of warm and friendly hospitality. There are seven rooms for travelers: five with one double bed, two with a double and a twin bed, and one with a double bed and set of trundle beds. Each room has a private bath. The hallways and some of the rooms are done in cypress panelling. All guest rooms are fully heated, centrally air conditioned, carpeted and include cable television. Morning coffee is provided.

The Combses will be delighted to suggest some good places to eat in the Kill Devil Hills area. They will also tell you about all the activities available for visitors—swimming, sailing, surfing, hang gliding, fishing, bicycling, kite flying and lots more. If you are not feeling all that energetic, simply relax and be lazy on the breeze-cooled porches in comfortable hammocks or chairs, or sun on the excellent beaches nearby.

Ye Olde Cherokee Inn, P.O. Box 315, Kill Devil Hills, NC 27948; (919) 441-6127. (Opposite Wright Brothers Monument on the beach road.) June through August (Memorial Day to Labor Day season): $25-$50 per night

GUEST HOUSES

for one or two persons, $3-$5 each additional person; rates for rest of year usually $50 per week. Major credit cards accepted during summer season; cash rest of year. No pets, please. Open year-around.

First Colony Inn. Betty B. Clarke, proprietor of this pleasant guest house in Nags Head, says that staying here is "a unique experience." The First Colony, built in 1932, is a cedar-shingled structure with a hip roof and wide, white-railinged porches. There are approximately six single, six double and six triple rooms for visitors, including efficiencies and separate cottages; all accommodations have private baths. In the lobby, guests will find a large selection of books and games, including backgammon played with seashells, and television.

A private beach is all yours for ocean swimming, body surfing, surf fishing, kite flying and volleyball. Hang gliding is available nearby, as is tennis on public courts. Or, you may simply sun on the beach or relax in a rocking chair on the porch. Midweek, Mrs. Clarke puts on a watermelon feast on the beach for her guests. No other food is served, but the house is within walking distance of several good restaurants. Ask your hostess to suggest some; also ask her about the house's ghosts—reportedly seen by past guests!

First Colony Inn, P.O. Box 938, Nags Head, NC 27959; (919) 441-7365. (Highway 158, Milepost 12.5 Nags Head.) Rates for two: room $38 daily, $245 weekly; twin efficiency $40 daily, $260 weekly; double efficiency $42 daily, $270 weekly. Two- and three-room apartments weekly $325 and $350; penthouse apartment $375; cottages $350 and $425. A deposit of 50 percent is required with reservations. Deposit refunds are made with one month's notice on apartments and cottages, two weeks on rooms and efficiencies; a $10 processing charge is assessed. Off-season rates: 30 percent off for May and September. Major credit cards, personal checks and cash are accepted. No pets, please. Open May through September.

Harbor View Tourist Home. Situated in the village of Ocracoke overlooking the waterfront, the Harbor View is operated by Helena W. Willis. The large, white, two-story structure was built in 1922. Ask Mrs. Willis to point out the beaded ceiling taken from the old house her grandfather built for her father before he was married. The land has belonged to her family for generations.

For guests there are two rooms with double bed, one room (facing the water) with a double and a single bed, and two rooms with two double beds; a bath down the hall is shared. Most of the furnishings in the house are antique; the airy rooms are, Mrs. Willis says, "just plain and simple." Parking is available. Nearby (about three-fourths of a mile) are great beaches for swimming or hiking; you can water ski in the tiny harbor, too. Mrs. Willis does not serve food, but there are restaurants within walking distance.

Harbor View Tourist Home, P.O. Box 243, Ocracoke, NC 27960; (919) 928-4501. (Ask Mrs. Willis to give you precise directions.) Rooms with double bed $16.64, room with double and single bed $18.72, rooms with two double beds $20.80. Cash or traveler's checks only. No pets or children, please. Open June through August.

Beach House. *Beach House* is an appropriate name for this attractive guest house by the sea, but it is really named for its owners, Tom and Carol Beach. Built in 1918 as a residence and tourist home by Walter C. O'Neal, a well-known hunting and fishing guide, the house remained in the O'Neal family until the Beaches purchased it in 1977. Since then they have been working hard to restore the two-story structure to its original state. It is a durable old place and has withstood many a blow throughout the years. During the storm of 1944, high tides actually entered the house; in order to keep the place from floating off its foundation, Mr. O'Neal cut a "float hole" in the floor of the master bedroom.

Beach House is located in Ocracoke, on Silver Lake (Ocracoke's scenic harbor). All the village's restaurants and shops are within easy walking distance, and there is free parking. The Beaches provide guests with breakfast, included in the rates. They will also serve dinner when requested; they specialize in freshly caught seafood and homemade breads. There are four rooms available for guests; all are air conditioned; the rooms share a bath.

Beach House, P.O. Box 443, Ocracoke, NC 27960; (919) 928-6471. (On N.C. 12, Silver Lake, Ocracoke.) Rates for two people in room, including breakfast; in summer $27 per room, off season $25 per room. No credit cards are accepted. No pets, please. Open year-around.

Blackbeard's Lodge. Luckily for guests, that old terror of a pirate Blackbeard is long gone. But his memory lives on in legend in Ocracoke, and if you are feeling romantic, you can indulge in fantasy to your heart's content in Blackbeard's Lodge. Mr. Doward H. Brugh is your genial host and a font of knowledge about Ocracoke Island and its colorful history.

The Lodge's main building was constructed in 1930 and remodeled in 1960; an annex was added in 1979. Parking is available on the premises. For guests there are nine two-bedroom efficiency apartments, three one-bedroom apartments, and 26 rooms with a double and single bed in each. All are air conditioned. Two sets of connecting rooms share a bath; all others have private baths. Each room is named after an exotic port, and every stair riser bears the name of a notorious pirate. The decor is nautical—designed around pirates, shipwrecks and buried treasure.

Mr. Brugh says that many of his guests return again and again and have become his good friends. The lodge is a most hospitable place and offers a relaxed, peaceful atmosphere. No food is served, but Mr. Brugh will be pleased to suggest a few good places to eat, including one just across the street. Nearby are 16 miles of beautiful, sandy beaches; they are free to all for swimming, surfing or fishing. Ask Mr. Brugh to point you in the direction of the lighthouse, oldest on the East Coast still in operation, and the herd of wild ponies, which are all descended from the original animals thought to have found their way here from the wreck of a Spanish ship centuries ago. Once the ponies roamed the island in great numbers; now the small herd that remains lives on a fenced-in range on the island's west side. *Blackbeard's Lodge, P.O. Box 37, Ocracoke, NC 27960; (919) 928-3421 or 928-9591. Summer rates $27.50-$42 per day depending on accommodations; winter rates $23.50-$36; additional person in room $5 per day. Summer rates apply to all holidays. Efficiencies sleep from four to six people; cribs, cots or floor mattresses are available for all rooms at an additional cost of $5 per day per person. No credit cards accepted; cash or personal checks only. Reservations are necessary; a deposit of one day's room rate is required, 50 percent for efficiency apartments. Fifteen days' notice is requested on deposit refunds. No pets, please. Open March through November.*

THE PIEDMONT REGION

The state's central Piedmont Plateau begins near Raleigh and continues all the way to the Blue Ridge Divide.

Northern Piedmont/Raleigh

Raleigh, North Carolina's capital, was laid out in 1792 and named for that courtly soldier, explorer and colonizer Sir Walter

Raleigh. According to local history, the state's legislators chose the site because it was only four miles from a popular tavern. Running a government can be a trying, throat-drying occupation, and the need for a soothing dram was once again catered to after the Civil War, during the Reconstruction period. A rowdy group of carpetbagger politicians set up their own bar in the Capitol, which still has nicks in its steps from the whiskey barrels rolled up to quench their thirst.

North Carolina's dynamic mix of industry (particularly tobacco, textiles and furniture) is most evident in the Piedmont region. Durham and Winston-Salem are both large tobacco centers. Durham (northwest of Raleigh) is also the home of Duke University. The University of North Carolina, oldest state university in the United States, is located in Chapel Hill, just beyond Durham. Founded in 1795, the institution's 2000-acre campus contains about 125 buildings, including the excellent Morehead Planetarium and Coker Arboretum. Greensboro, a few miles further north, is the hometown of O. Henry (William Sydney Porter) the famed American author of short stories.

Guilford Courthouse National Military Park is six miles northwest of Greensboro. Here Lord Cornwallis won a battle in 1781, but lost so many men doing it that his weakened British forces were defeated seven months later in Yorktown. There is a self-guided, two-mile walking trail through the battleground; the Visitor Center offers descriptive films and displays.

Continuing west you will come to Winston-Salem. Old Salem, a restored eighteenth-century Moravian community, provides a fascinating glimpse into an unusual way of life. More than thirty of the original structures have been restored; early crafts are demonstrated in the Single Brothers House, built in 1769. The Moravians emigrated from Germany in 1735; they set up their first community in America in Savannah, Georgia. Six years later they moved to Pennsylvania, and in 1766 a group moved back to the South to found Salem. (Salem merged with the neighboring town of Winston in 1913.)

The Moravian faith was a strict one in the 1700s, but far from dull. Its followers loved bright colors, music and good food. At Christmastime in Old Salem visitors are invited to sample the traditional Moravian sugar buns and *Lebkuchen*, holiday cookies made with honey, almonds and orange peel, at Candle Teas held in the Single Brothers House. While you nibble, you can watch beeswax candles being dipped for the Christmas Eve

GUEST HOUSES

Love Feast services. At Easter, visitors are welcome to attend the Sunrise Service that begins in Salem Square in front of the Home Church and ends in the Moravian cemetery, called God's Acre. Its more than 4000 gravestones are all scrubbed white and decorated with fresh flowers.

Restover Tourist Home. Located in old Raleigh, this handsome three-story Greek Revival house was built in 1872. Mrs. Edith Weems, a gracious, friendly lady originally from New England, will be delighted to show you around. Notice the living room with its 20-foot ceiling and teakwood fireplace, the original gas light fixtures, and the winding stairs with art nouveau stained-glass windows. Restover is a homey sort of place, with a most pleasant atmosphere. And the rates are extremely reasonable.

There are five attractively decorated guest rooms with accommodations for singles or doubles; all have fireplaces and private baths. No meals are served, but there are all manner of restaurants within walking distance. The Governor's Mansion is three blocks away, and many other points of interest in Raleigh are close by, such as the North Carolina Museum of History and the State Capitol. Parking is available in Mrs. Weems' six-car garage behind the house.

Restover Tourist Home, 506 N. Person Street, Raleigh, NC 27605; (919) 828-1579. Single $9; double $12. Cash accepted or personal checks with identification. Guests should have luggage and an automobile. No pets, please. Open year-around.

Restover Tourist Home, Raleigh, N.C.

Southern Piedmont/Pinehurst

In the southern Piedmont, horses and golf predominate in the gently rolling, piney region known as the Sandhills. Two year-around resorts, Southern Pines and Pinehurst, have become world famous for both equestrian sports and superb golf. Southern Pines is the home of North Carolina's oldest organized hunt, the Moore County Hounds. During the winter months, the members regularly ride out on fox and drag hunts. In early April Southern Pines hosts the Stoneybrook Steeplechase Races. Pinehurst offers the World Golf Hall of Fame (on Gerald R. Ford Blvd.) with displays portraying the history of golf, along with photographs of famous golfers and other memorabilia. The Colgate-Hall of Fame Golf Classic is held at the Pinehurst Country Club every August.

If neither horses nor whacking away at a small white ball appeal to you, there are also excellent tennis and hunting and a great number of shops offering a dazzling array of posh items, plus some fine native handcrafts. There is also a splendid nature area, the Weymouth Woods–Sandhills Nature Preserve, with a museum of natural history and miles of hiking trails along the pine-covered "sandridges." Carowinds, a colorful theme park, is located on the North/South Carolina border ten miles south of Charlotte (about a two-hour drive west of the Pinehurst region). Its seven historical theme areas illustrate the culture and heritage of the two Carolinas; there are loads of marvelous rides, and for families, especially, it is lots of fun.

Pinehurst is not actually a town, but a privately owned corporation. Founded in 1845, it was the brainchild of James Walker Tufts, a Boston philanthropist. His idea was to create a retreat for fellow Northerners who might wish to escape the snow and ice of winter. Tufts asked Frederick Law Olmsted, the renowned landscape architect, to design the place. Olmsted created a charming village that combines the lush greenery and flowers of the South with the traditional ambiance of New England (there is even a village green). Pinehurst is an elegant and quite expensive resort. There is, however, a perfectly splendid guest house. Not only is it located right in the center of Pinehurst Village, but its extremely reasonable rates include a complete breakfast!

The Magnolia Inn. The beautiful old, rambling and comfortable Magnolia Inn has a long front porch on the ground level and an even longer one running around the second floor. The house was built in 1896 by the Tufts family, founders of Pinehurst; the white-painted structure has always been used as a guest house. The present owner, Leslie Wilson, purchased it about 14 years ago and runs it with the help of two daughters.

Accommodations include one single, nine double, and three triple rooms for guests; all have private baths, twin beds and air conditioning. There is a swimming pool on the lovely tree-shaded grounds for summer use, and in the wintertime guests are invited to sit around a crackling fire in the living room. Plenty of parking is available; excellent restaurants and shops are within walking distance. Horseback riding and tennis are both available nearby. And as a guest at Magnolia Inn, you are invited to play golf at the prestigious Pinehurst Country Club on any of its six magnificent eighteen-hole courses.

The Magnolia Inn, P.O. Box 266, Magnolia Road, Pinehurst, NC 28374; (919) 295-6900. Rates: $14 per person per day including breakfast. Cash, personal checks with identification and traveler's checks accepted; no credit cards. No pets allowed (a North Carolina state law), but children are welcome. Open year-around.

The Magnolia Inn, Pinehurst, N.C.

NORTH CAROLINA'S MOUNTAINS

The western portion of North Carolina is one of extravagant beauty—of ancient, blue-hazed mountains and deep valleys, spectacular waterfalls and white-water gorges, quaint mountain towns and an ever-changing display of flowers and foliage. The best way to explore the region is to follow the Blue Ridge Parkway. The parkway starts in Virginia's Shenandoah National Forest and ends at Cherokee, North Carolina, where the Great Smoky Mountains National Forest begins. The parkway is dotted with overlooks; each one seems to offer a more superb view than the last. There are hiking trails galore and camping sites and a host of things to see and do that are easily reached from the parkway.

Old highland farms are visible sometimes, too, with their weathered cabins and barns and split-rail fences. In the towns adjacent to the parkway, you will find the descendants of the original settlers and a way of life that still includes many of the old traditional customs.

The mountains are magnificent year-around. In late April, dogwood blooms in white drifts. Later on, purple rhododendron, flame-colored azaleas and delicately tinted mountain laurel cover the hillsides. In autumn the trees blaze with vivid reds, yellows and oranges, contrasting with the dark green of firs. Except when winter snow or ice and occasional summer fog cause temporary shut-downs, the parkway is open all year.

The sharp-eyed traveler will be able to spot an abundance of wildlife along the road—chipmunks, skunks, foxes and raccoons. White-tailed deer usually stay deep within the forest, but may sometimes be observed near the road at dawn or dusk. Bears, too, may appear at these times, but they are unpredictable.

Do not try to feed a bear, even if it does look amiable. Bears do not know the difference between a sandwich and your arm. Also, if you stop for a picnic beside a mountain stream or take a hike along a trail, be sure to tightly close your car's doors and windows. Bears are clever creatures, quite capable of climbing in after your food supply. It can be a nasty shock to return to your vehicle and find it occupied by a very large, furry beast. A surprised bear will usually run away. (So will a surprised human.) But with bears, one never knows for sure.

Beginning at the northern end of the North Carolina section of the Blue Ridge Parkway and heading south, you will come to

GUEST HOUSES

the area called The High South, which includes the towns of Boone, Blowing Rock, Banner Elk and Linville. They're all enormously popular summer vacation resorts, but they also offer excellent winter skiing facilities. (Snow-makers are used when natural snow refuses to fall.) Throughout the region are handicraft shops by the dozens where you can buy such fascinating items as strip-oak baskets, corn-shuck dolls, fireplace brooms, mountain toys and musical instruments, quilts, rustic furniture and hand-turned pottery. There are some interesting guest houses, too, ranging from traditional family homes to contemporary chalets.

Boone

The town of Boone is named for Daniel Boone, who lived in a cabin here in the 1760s. One mile east of town, you can visit the Daniel Boone Native Gardens, an extensive collection of native plants and flowers in a natural setting. The gates to the gardens were made by one of Boone's descendants, Daniel VI. While you're here, attend a performance of *Horn in the West*, an exciting drama held in an outdoor amphitheater on the same grounds as the gardens. Back in 1776 when the Blue Ridge Mountains marked the frontier, American colonists "heard a horn blowing in the West." The "horn" called them to battle with the British forces and their fierce Indian allies. The story relates that from deep in the mountains of western North Carolina the people responded, including a group led by Daniel Boone. The mountaineers surrounded and engaged the British troops and defeated them soundly. *Horn in the West* is presented nightly except Mondays from late June through late August.

The Beckon Ridge. The Beckon Ridge is a two-story white house, about 50 years old, with a big front porch and a nice yard with lots of birds and flowers. Mrs. Margaret Herndon is your gracious hostess. The six guest rooms include two rooms with twin beds, one with a double bed and three with two twins and a double. Two baths are shared. There is no television and no air conditioning, but Mrs. Herndon sometimes entertains guests by playing the piano and the mountain air keeps rooms delightfully cool. No food is served; there are, however, plenty of restaurants nearby. Since parking is available on the premises, you can leave your car and walk to just about everything in town.

The Beckon Ridge, 400 Hardin Street, Boone, NC 28607; (704) 264-2327. (Corner of Pine Street and U.S. 321.) Rates: $15 for one, $20 for two, and $25 for three or four persons. No pets, no alcohol, please. Open June 1 to August 15.

Ole Waterloo. Mrs. Jennie Greene, who is 81 years old, has a delightful story of how her guest house got its unusual name. It seems that a creek runs under the house and used to flood the place from time to time. Before Mrs. Greene bought the place in 1965 and installed drainpipes for the water to run through, the house had defeated every owner—like Napoleon at *his* Waterloo!

Today the house is dry and cozy, an attractive stone-sided house set amidst mountain firs. There is a comfortable front porch for relaxing outdoors and plenty of parking space. Mrs. Greene has six guest rooms, including accommodations for singles, doubles and triples. There are one private and two semi-private baths. Generally, no food is served (there are many restaurants in the area), but Mrs. Greene will fix breakfast for you if you ask in advance. Guests are also allowed to use the kitchen if they wish.

Ole Waterloo was built in 1910 and therefore is old enough to have a resident ghost. Although Mrs. Greene was told by previous owners that a ghost walked the house at night, she has never seen it. If you have an affinity with the spirit world, you might be lucky enough to meet the walker. If not, just ignore the whole thing.

Ole Waterloo, P.O. Box 30, Boone, NC 28607; (704) 264-8034. (Located one mile west of Boone Police Station on U.S. 421.) Rates are given on request; they will be very reasonable. Open year-around.

Blowing Rock

From Boone, take U.S. 321 south a few miles to Blowing Rock. Along the way, you will want to stop for a ride on the Tweetsie Railroad. The chuffing, tooting, authentic old coal-fired locomotive pulls open-air coaches on a three-mile trip during which the train is "attacked" by Indians and train robbers. The Tweetsie Railroad setting includes a re-creation of a Western town, a chairlift ride to Mouse Mountain, a visit to the Tweetsie Mining Co., the Mouse Mine Ride, gold panning, a petting zoo and much more, including a magic show at Tweetsie Palace.

GUEST HOUSES

You might also enjoy a stop at Mystery Hill nearby, where water and balls run uphill in the Mystery House and you seem to be standing at an impossible angle. It is hokey, but fun. For serious folks, the adjacent Antique Museum has a fascinating clutter of items used in the old days in these mountains.

A resort for more than 80 years, the town of Blowing Rock was named for a nearby cliff that overhangs Johns River Gorge 3000 feet below. Any light object (such as a handkerchief) thrown over the edge of the rock will float right back up to you. There is a romantic Indian legend about the phenomenon: long ago, it is said, a young Cherokee brave leaped from the rock to return to his tribe in the wilderness far below. (It may have seemed the shortest route.) His sweetheart, the daughter of a Chickasaw chieftain, was grief stricken, believing that her lover had died in the fall. Nevertheless, she prayed daily to the Great Spirit, asking for her hero's return. Then, the legend continues, on an evening with a reddening sky a sudden gust of wind blew the young man back onto the rock and into her arms. And from that day, a perpetual wind has blown up onto the rock from the valley below.

The stark scientific explanation is that the rocky walls of the gorge form a flume through which the northwest wind sweeps with such force that it returns light objects cast out over the void. Even so, it is still impressive . . . in wintertime even the snow seems to fall upside down.

Maple Lodge. A really delightful guest house, Maple Lodge was included in the 1980 Blowing Rock Annual Tour of Homes. (The Tour ended with a picnic luncheon on the church lawn; each guest received a miniature peach basket containing quiche, salad and lemon cake.)

Jack and Rheba Crane purchased Maple Lodge in 1979. The house was built in 1946 and is surrounded by trees, shrubbery and a nice lawn. You can sit in the comfortable wicker lawn chairs and breathe in the mountain air. The lodge's decor is turn-of-the-century "Grandmother's House"; the Cranes continue to search out and add pieces of old oak furniture and other treasures. One of their more recent acquisitions is an old pipe organ.

Each of the eight guest rooms in the main house has a private bath. There is also a two-bedroom cottage on the grounds, with two baths. Guests are invited to use the two parlors and large

Maple Lodge, Blowing Rock, N.C.

"Florida" room in the lodge; on chilly evenings there is a cheery blaze going in the small parlor's stone fireplace. A Continental breakfast of juice, fruit, muffins or breakfast breads and coffee or milk is included in the rates.

Maple Lodge is just off Main Street and within walking distance of restaurants, shops and churches. The Blue Ridge Parkway is a mile away. The Cranes will gladly suggest things to do in the area, such as horseback riding, hiking and snow skiing. Parking is available at the house.

It seems appropriate here to quote a local resident, Mrs. Mary Beck, concerning the community of Blowing Rock and Maple Lodge. She says: "We old-time residents [she's 88] have until recently kept to 'the mountain atmosphere,' but our influx of newcomers is trying to make the place 'citified.' People come here because they like the quiet atmosphere and think it would be a nice place to live—then, after they get here they try to make it like the place they come from!" Maple Lodge, she notes, is special. "It's truly a lovely place, and Blowing Rock never had anything so elegant. I can heartily recommend it and feel that anyone who stays in this charming house will be delighted."

Maple Lodge, P.O. Box 66, Sunset Drive, Blowing Rock, NC 28605; (704) 295-3331. (Next to Blowing Rock Elementary School.) Single $30 a

GUEST HOUSES

night; double $35; each additional person $5 (all including breakfast). Cash or personal checks; no credit cards. No pets, but children are welcome. Open year-around.

Sunshine Inn. A porch complete with rocking chairs and a swing fronts old, country-style Sunshine Inn. Indoors, the slanted floors tend to squeak cozily as one treads on them. Jim and Sue Byrne are the new owners of Sunshine Inn and plan to make it an old-fashioned bed-and-breakfast type of operation, possibly with dinner as an option.

The Byrnes have seven guest rooms—six doubles and two with twin beds, sharing two baths. Parking is available at the house. Restaurants, shops and various points of interest in Blowing Rock are within walking distance.

Sunshine Inn, Sunset Drive, Blowing Rock, NC 28605; (704) 295-3487. Rates range from $19 to $28. Personal checks or cash accepted. No pets, please. Open year-around.

Grandfather Mountain and Banner Elk

From Blowing Rock, U.S. 221 will bring you to Linville and Grandfather Mountain. This ancient mountain is 5964 feet high with a steep, winding road leading to its summit. Along the way you will see rock formations said to be a billion years old. Up on top there is a scary but safe swinging bridge to walk across from one peak to another and an unbeatable 360-degree view of the region. An environmental habitat is home for a group of bears, including the famed Mildred and—sometimes—her cubs. There is another habitat for deer. Hang-gliding flights take off from Grandfather Mountain, weather permitting, from May to October. "Singing on the Mountain," a lively presentation of traditional and modern gospel music, is performed here on the fourth Sunday in June, and on the second weekend of July the mountain hosts the Highland Games and Gathering of Scottish Clans.

Drive a few miles south to Linville Gorge and its spectacular falls. The Linville River, one of North Carolina's wildest white-water streams, originates high on the slopes of Grandfather Mountain. It drops more than 2000 feet through the gorge's 12-mile stretch of deep, curving canyon, part of the 7600-acre Linville Gorge Wilderness Area.

Linville Caverns are also in this region, on U.S. 221 between Linville and Marion. Open year-around, the caverns (discovered about 100 years ago) run under the mountain.

Deserters from both armies were said to have used them as hiding places during the Civil War. Guides lead visitors through the caves, which have (as all good caverns do) stalactite and stalagmite formations and other natural wonders. Unfortunately, the formations have been dubbed with fanciful names by the management.

Heading north from Grandfather Mountain on N.C. 184, you will come to Banner Elk, a bustling ski resort in winter and home of The Land of Oz in summer. The Land of Oz is a delightful walk-through theme park reached by a 4000-foot chairlift (there are buses, too) running from Beech Tree Village. Kids will love following the Yellow Brick Road accompanied by the Wicked Witch and other Oz characters. Youthful visitors can experience Dorothy's tornado, ride "back to Kansas" in her giant balloon and explore the Wizard of Oz museum.

Top of the Beech Inn. Ute and Barry Wolfgang's Beech Inn offers the highest guest accommodations, at 5020 feet, in the Southeastern United States. The inn is not a typical guest house, but an Alpine chalet-style structure with exposed beams, built in 1960. For travelers there are fourteen rooms with two double beds, eight with queen-size beds, and one efficiency apartment with a double bed. Each room has a private bath. Included in the rates is a Continental breakfast of coffee, juice and rolls. An excellent restaurant about 200 feet away serves breakfast and dinner, and Beech Tree Village (with eating places, shops and ski lifts) is about a mile away. Beech Mountain offers excellent snow and grass skiing; ice skating, swimming, golf and tennis are all available within a mile or two.

Top of the Beech Inn, Route 2, Banner Elk, NC 28604; (704) 387-2252. (On top of Beech Mountain, well marked, the first large building on the traveler's right.) Rates for double rooms begin at $48; please inquire for details. Major credit cards, cash and checks for advance deposit accepted. No pets. Open year-around.

Beech Alpen Inn, Ltd. Beech Alpen, sister to Top of the Beech Inn, is also a departure from the usual definition of a guest house. Owners Dori Wallace and Jeff Alberts say: "It was originally built as sort of a retirement 'hobby.' The first owner really went all out with the furnishings . . . creating a luxurious 'inn' atmosphere. Even though Beech Alpen is only 12 years old, the way it was constructed makes it seem much older."

The architecture is Old World, with heavy beamed ceilings,

stucco walls and Mediterranean-style furniture. Four corner guest rooms each have their own fireplace, and steambath, too. In addition, there are 17 double and four single rooms without fireplaces. All the rooms have private baths and separate vanities, color television, phone and piped-in music. A Continental breakfast of juice, coffee and Danish, included in the rates, is served each morning in the comfortable lounge. During winter ski season, a buffet supper is also available.

Recreational facilities on Beech Mountain include golf, tennis, an Olympic-size pool for summer swimming, hiking, winter ice-skating and both snow and grass skiing.

Beech Alpen Inn, Ltd., Route 2, Beech Mountain, Banner Elk, NC 28604; (704) 387-2261. (Located atop Beech Mountain.) Summer rates: fireplace rooms $38; rooms with two double beds $38; rooms with one double bed $32. Winter rates: fireplace rooms $64; rooms with two double beds $54; rooms with one double bed $44. Major credit cards, cash and personal checks with two forms of identification accepted. Children are most welcome. Open year-around.

Minneapolis

Appalachian Inn. Southwest of Banner Elk, there is a tiny village called Minneapolis, set deep in the North Carolina mountains. The Appalachian Inn in Minneapolis is not truly a guest house for it does serve meals, but because of its amazingly low rates ($15 including breakfast and dinner) it has been included. We thought you would like to know about it.

Owned by Mrs. Milton Vance, the house was built just before the turn of the century; it is really an old farm house set on more than an acre of land. Back in the old days, since there were no hotel accommodations close by, Mrs. Vance's mother, the late Phoebe Y. Burleson, decided to open her home to overnight guests. The place has been going ever since.

There are ten rooms for visitors, including three singles and seven doubles; and there are seven bathrooms. Breakfast is served at 8:30 a.m., dinner at 7 p.m. Mrs. Vance specializes in old-fashioned country cooking—country ham, fresh garden vegetables and the like.

The house is in a lovely, quiet, peaceful area; it's a marvelous place to relax for a time and soak up the mountain atmosphere. Grandfather Mountain and Mount Mitchell are both nearby, as are miles of hiking trails. There is a swimming pool right across the street, and restaurants and shops are about three miles away.

*Appalachian Inn, P.O. Box 24, Minneapolis, NC 28652; (704) 733-4070
or 733-2798. (Located on U.S. 19E.) Rates: $15 per day including
breakfast and dinner. Cash is preferred; no credit cards. No pets, please.
Open June 15 to October.*

Asheville and Brevard

Back on the Blue Ridge Parkway again, you will come to Mt.
Mitchell State Park (just off the Parkway on N.C. 128). There is
an auto road to the summit of Mount Mitchell itself. The peak
rises 6684 feet (the highest point east of the Mississippi River)
and has an incomparable view of North Carolina's other mountains and valleys.

Next, the Parkway swoops down south of Asheville. There
you can visit the Thomas Wolfe Memorial, 40 Spruce Street,
maintained by the state as a literary shrine. The renowned
novelist grew up in Asheville; he lived in this rambling Victorian home, which his mother ran as a boarding house. In his
book *Look Homeward, Angel,* the house was called Dixieland.
Both Wolfe and O. Henry are buried in Asheville's Riverside
Cemetery.

The absolute opposite of a simple rooming house is the
Biltmore House, two miles south of Asheville on U.S. 25 off
I-40. The Biltmore House is situated on an 11,000-acre estate
and has 35 acres of formal gardens laid out by Frederick Law
Olmsted. More than 500 varieties of azaleas are grown here;
there is also a four-acre Walled Garden, said to be the finest
English garden in America.

The 250-room French Renaissance chateau was
designed by Richard Morris Hunt for George W. Vanderbilt. Its
most interesting and best-furnished rooms are open to visitors,
and they are splendid indeed. Completed in 1896 by workers
and artisans from all over the world, the chateau holds an
almost endless list of treasures: Napoleon's chess set; prints by
Durer and Landseer; Portuguese, Spanish and Italian
eighteenth- and nineteenth-century furnishings; portraits by
Sargent and Whistler and much, much more.

The 72- by 42-foot Banquet Hall arches 75 feet high and is
graced with two late nineteenth-century Gothic thrones and
five rare middle sixteenth-century Flemish tapestries. The
library, with more than 20,000 volumes, has a magnificent
painted ceiling attributed to Pellegrini; one bedroom is panelled
in walnut, and another's walls are covered with yellow silk. But

GUEST HOUSES

it would take an entire book to describe the Biltmore House; you must see it for yourself to appreciate its stunning grandeur. The house and gardens are open year-around except Thanksgiving, Christmas and New Year's Day. A prize herd of dairy cows is maintained on part of the property, and there is a dairy bar where you can purchase a snack, and perhaps even see a modern-day Vanderbilt in the flesh.

If you are in Asheville during the summer, you are invited to take part in some of North Carolina's finest presentations of country dancing and music. Shindig-on-the-Green takes place in front of city hall Saturday evenings in July and August (except for the first weekend in August when the Mountain Dance and Folk Festival is held). You can listen to mountain fiddlers, dulcimer players and singers performing traditional folk songs and ballads, or you can swing your partner in a rollicking session of square dancing.

In Brevard, south of Asheville, the Summer Festival of Music offers symphonic, choral, chamber and operatic performances; they are presented from late June to early August. Over in Flat Rock, about 30 miles southwest of Asheville, you can visit Carl Sandburg's home and farm where the famed poet, writer and historian lived for more than two decades. In the same area, the North Carolina State Theater's Flat Rock Playhouse presents a series of dramas from late June through August.

"The Dunlops'." Located in a quiet neighborhood in Brevard, Mr. and Mrs. Charles S. Dunlop's guest house is a newer home, a comfortable two-story frame house built in 1948. It is surrounded by beautiful shrubs and flowers, and there is an outdoor picnic grill for cook-outs. The house is furnished in antiques and has two guest rooms with double beds and one room with twin beds. Guests share one and a half bathrooms. No food is served, but there are plenty of restaurants within walking distance. Parking is available at the house.

The Dunlops', 212 Park View Drive, Brevard, NC 28712; (704) 883-9292. (From center of town turn left off East Main Street at Park Avenue; then, after two blocks, turn right onto Park View Drive.) Rates: $15 per day per room; weekly $35. Cash or personal checks with identification; no credit cards. Children are welcome; there is no charge for those under 10. And the Dunlops will make arrangements for pets. Open year-around.

Bay-Horse Farm. Bay-Horse Farm is a really unusual sort of "guest house"—an authentic mountain cabin with all the modern conveniences! If you would really like to escape the city, be on your own and just contemplate Nature, you can rent the cozy place by the week. It's located about 25 miles from Brevard.

Mr. and Mrs. G. O. Shepherd own Bay-Horse Farm; it was built about 60 years ago by native mountain people and modernized by the Shepherds. It has three bedrooms, bath, large kitchen and a living room with fireplace. Linens, dishes and pots and pans are furnished. You just bring food and yourself.

The property borders part of the Pisgah National Forest, which has miles of hiking and horseback-riding trails. There is even a small lake for fishing and swimming. The picturesque drive out to the cabin crosses a tumbling, clear mountain stream complete with fish. There are no restaurants or shops or the like nearby, and that's the charm of the place.

G. O. Shepherd, Rte. 1, Brevard, NC 28712; (704) 862-4896. The Shepherds will give you directions for reaching the cabin (it is about 7 miles from U.S. 64, on N.C. 281 past Lake Toxaway). Will not sleep more than seven or eight persons. A deposit of $65 per week is requested. Cash or personal checks accepted; no credit cards. Available May 31 to October 31.

Bay-Horse Farm, Brevard N.C.

GUEST HOUSES

Cherokee and Robbinsville

The Blue Ridge Parkway comes to an end at Cherokee. If you are heading for Tennessee, take U.S. 441 through the Great Smoky Mountains National Park to Gatlinburg and beyond; it is a superlatively beautiful drive. If you're heading south to Georgia, follow U.S. 19. The Joyce Kilmer/Slick Rock Wilderness Area, which lies northwest of Robbinsville in the Nantahala National Forest, is a popular place for hiking and backpacking, hunting and fishing.

Whichever way you go, stop in Cherokee for a visit. The descendants of the Cherokee people who escaped being forcibly marched to Oklahoma over the tragic "Trail of Tears" in the mid-1800s still live here on their own reservation. To see how the Cherokees lived 200 years ago, explore the Oconaluftee Indian Village. It is open to visitors from mid-May to late October, and you can watch Indians in traditional tribal dress making log canoes, weaving baskets or creating exquisite beadwork. The Museum of the Cherokee Indian (open all year) has arts, crafts, audiovisual displays and prehistoric artifacts. Both the village and the museum are located on U.S. 441, just north of Cherokee.

From late June through August, nightly except Sundays, the moving drama *Unto These Hills* is presented at Mountainside Theatre, a natural amphitheater next to the Oconaluftee Indian Village. The play ought not to be missed; it relates the history of the Cherokee Nation from 1540 to 1838. Also in the area is a more commercial venture, Frontier Land, on U.S. 19. Here you can wander through re-created pioneer and Indian villages and a fort, take a stagecoach or steam locomotive ride and watch Indian dances and shows. Frontier Land is open from May to October.

Wilsons' Tourist Home. Located in Robbinsville, southwest of Cherokee, this guest house is an old-timer. Thomas and Mellie Wilson have been in the business of welcoming travelers to their home for many years and say that they have thoroughly enjoyed every day of it. Their ten guest rooms have private or semi-private baths. The house has a large porch and shady lawn, and there is a cook-out shed for guests to use. And the rates are *extremely* reasonable.

Robbinsville is close to the Joyce Kilmer Forest, Nantahala Gorge and several large man-made lakes. The area offers great fishing, canoe and raft trips, hiking and picnicking. No food is served at the Wilsons, but at least four restaurants are within walking distance of the house. Plenty of parking is available.

Wilson's Tourist Home, Circle Street, P.O. Box 47. Robbinsville, NC 28771; (704) 479-8679. (Just off U.S. 129, in town, below the telephone tower.) Average rates $6-$9 per day, lower for longer stays. Visa and MasterCard accepted. No pets, but children are very welcome. Open year-around.

South Carolina

From its Atlantic beaches and offshore islands to the Blue Ridge Mountains in its northeast corner, South Carolina is a beautiful state. For the vacationer, it offers a marvelously diverse assortment of attractions: sports, amusements and festivals of all kinds, an abundance of historic sites and houses, magnificent, world-renowned gardens and a benign, temperate climate year-around.

Spanish explorers were the first Europeans to visit the region; they sailed along the coast of South Carolina in the early 1500s. Later in that century, two coastal colonies were established, one by the Spanish and another by French Huguenots; but both were soon abandoned. In 1629 England granted the enormous tract of land to a British nobleman, Sir Robert Heath. He failed to do anything with it, however, so King Charles II turned the territory (called Carolina) over to a group of eight Lords Proprietors in 1663. They later divided the grant into North and South Carolina.

The first permanent English settlement in South Carolina was founded in 1670 and called *Charles Town* after the king. (It was renamed Charleston in 1783.) The tiny colony was first located at Albemarle Point on the west bank of the Ashley River. Ten years later it was moved to the present site, a peninsula between the Ashley and Cooper rivers.

Charleston was, from the first, a patrician community of wealthy planters who established a gracious, formal way of life—a New World version of English aristocracy. Inland, settlers from Scotland, Ireland, Wales and Germany struggled with a very different kind of existence, wresting farmland from the rugged, hostile wilderness. The disparity between the two groups created a feeling of rancor, which did not die out until the mid-1800s. Charleston was South Carolina's capital for many years, and although the upcountry settlers outnumbered the coastal planters, the power to run the region's affairs lay entirely with the latter. The outlanders felt, with reason, that they were not properly represented. Even though they paid the same taxes, they were virtually ignored and received no help when it was needed—to fight off attacking Indians, for instance.

A truce was called, more or less, during the American Revolution. In 1775 Charleston was the first Southern city to defy the English by joining the revolutionary movement. The royal governor was forced to flee, and in 1776 South Carolina adopted the first independent state constitution. The British fleet attacked Charleston and captured the city in 1780; they held it for two years. Their victory did them little good, though. General Nathanael Greene's Continental troops, along with South Carolina patriots, kept the British pretty well boxed in, unable to move northward to join the other royal forces. Elsewhere in South Carolina, colonists were beating the tar out of the British in the battles of Kings Mountain and Cowpens.

The long-standing hassle over representation between up-country and lowcountry factions came to a head again shortly after the end of the Revolution. The upcountry citizens finally won out; in 1786 the capital was moved from Charleston to the geographical center of the state, where the city of Columbia was founded. The move did not end South Carolina's long history of contentiousness concerning unfair taxation, however. The state, its citizens now united, next took on the federal government.

In 1828 John Caldwell Calhoun, then Vice President of the United States, wrote an essay called *The South Carolina Exposition*. It opposed the government's tariff policy, which he thought favored the industrial North over the slave-holding South. The outcome was a compromise between the state and federal governments, and the tariff was reduced. But when Abraham Lincoln was elected President in 1860, South Carolina (led by Calhoun) became the first state to secede from the Union.

A year later, South Carolinians attacked the federal troops at Fort Sumter in Charleston harbor, setting off the Civil War. By 1868, when South Carolina rejoined the Union, the state was a blackened ruin, victim of General Sherman's march to the sea. Not until recent years did it really recover from the economic troubles resulting from the war and its aftermath. The combination of agriculture with a great influx of industry lured by the state's vast waterpower projects, an accessible labor force and low tax rates has turned South Carolina's economy around. Today it is one of the most prosperous states in the South.

Geographically, South Carolina can be divided into three regions: the Up Country of mountains and foothills; the Midlands, a gently rising plateau running down the center of the state; and the Low Country, a flat coastal plain fringed by Atlantic beaches, bays, inlets and sandy offshore islands.

THE UP COUNTRY

Up Country offers crisp, cool air and such superb scenery as a section of the Blue Ridge Mountains, rolling foothills and wild, white-water rivers. If you can, take the Cherokee Foothills Scenic Highway (S.C. 11), one of the state's most beautiful routes; it winds in a wide crescent for 130 miles. The road is spectacular in the spring when blooming dogwood resembles snowdrifts on the hillsides; in the fall the hills are aflame with the colors of autumn.

Cowpens National Battlefield, at the start of the highway near Gaffney, is the scene of General Daniel Morgan's victory over superior British forces on January 17, 1781; the battle is considered by many historians to have been a major turning point in the American Revolution. Kings Mountain National Military Park is 17 miles northeast of Gaffney, off I-85. There untrained mountain men of the Carolinas, Virginia and Georgia managed, against great odds, to break up the British push to the south. Kings Mountain State Park is just on the southern edge—for hiking, swimming and boating.

If you would like to experience real wilderness, head a few miles west of the Scenic Highway to the Chattooga River. The river begins on the crest of the Blue Ridge Mountains in North Carolina, then runs along the borders of South Carolina and Georgia, joining the Tugaloo to form the great Savannah River. Dropping an average of 49.3 feet per mile, the untamed Chattooga tumbles down a 40-mile stretch of rapids and narrow rock flumes, sometimes quieting into wide, deep pools and calm, wadeable shallows. You can canoe parts of it or take a white-water raft trip. There are miles of fine hiking trails in the region, too.

The city of Greenville, east of the Scenic Highway, is worth a side trip to see its fine art collections. The Bob Jones University Art Museum houses rare Biblical materials and sacred art including works by Botticelli, Rubens and Rembrandt. The Greenville County Museum of Art has the most complete collection anywhere of Andrew Wyeth's work. In 1979 Arthur and Holly Magill purchased 26 Wyeth paintings from movie magnate Joseph E. Levine for $4.5 million. They then bought 260 works from Wyeth's personal collection for another $3 to $5 million and donated them all to the Greenville Museum.

THE MIDLANDS

Columbia is the star of South Carolina's Midlands region. The state capital since 1786, Columbia was one of the country's first planned cities, laid out in a checkerboard pattern with exceptionally broad, tree-lined streets. Pay a visit to the Columbia Museum of Art and Science to view the superb collection of Renaissance paintings and sculpture, plus contemporary graphics, a wonderful gallery of dolls and fascinating science displays. Columbia's Riverbanks Zoo opened in 1974; it is one of the newest and finest zoological parks in the world. Wide moats, water and light form natural barriers that allow the more than 700 types of mammals and birds to live in their appropriate environments. Columbia is also home of the South Carolina State Fair, held in late October.

Camden, northeast of Columbia, is South Carolina's oldest inland city. It was founded in 1732 and was the major British garrison during the Revolution, commanded by Lord Cornwallis. More than a dozen Revolutionary War battles were fought in the area, and Camden itself was burned by the British when they evacuated it in 1781. The city is also noted for its equestrian sports and races. South of Columbia is Aiken, center of Carolina's thoroughbred country. Polo matches, harness racing, thoroughbred trials and steeplechase and hunt meets are all held in this fashionable resort area during winter and spring months.

THE LOW COUNTRY

The coastal plain Low Country of South Carolina begins at the northeast tip of the state. The Grand Strand, some 60 miles of broad, sandy beaches, runs along the coast from Myrtle Beach down to Georgetown. All along the way are warm-water swimming, surfing, fishing, great seafood and a host of family activities. Starting with Georgetown, founded in 1729, you will find yourself easing into South Carolina's romantic past. Further south along the coast comes the seaport of Charleston, enchanting with its elegant air, rows of lovely old houses and flowers. Nearby are several of the state's fabulous gardens.

South of Charleston, the coastline becomes a watery region of inlets, sea marshes and semi-tropical offshore islands. On

Port Royal Island is Beaufort, one of South Carolina's prettiest and most historic towns (and the second oldest). Spanish explorers discovered Beaufort's harbor in 1520; the first Protestant colony on the American continent was founded here in 1562 by French Huguenots; and Spanish, English and Scottish colonies, all short-lived, followed. The present city was founded in 1710 and named after the Duke of Beaufort. (It is pronounced "Bewfort," by the way.) Hilton Head Island, now a popular resort, was discovered in 1663 by the English explorer Captain William Hilton. Hunting Island State Park has 5000 acres of beaches, forests and marshes and a 136-foot-high lighthouse to climb for a fabulous view of the surrounding area.

Mullins

Tobacco is big business in South Carolina, and the Mullins area northwest of coastal Myrtle Beach offers a host of tobacco auctions from mid-July to September 1. Children and grownups, too, will be fascinated by the auctioneer's fast-paced chants. In the towns of Conway and Loris, hostesses are on duty at the tobacco warehouses during the selling season from 9 a.m. to 12 noon, Monday through Thursday, to explain the auctioning procedures.

Webster Manor, Mullins, S.C.

GUEST HOUSES

Webster Manor. This handsome old house in Mullins was built in 1903. A Colonial with a wide front porch, the house is large and rambling and surrounded by flowers, trees and shrubbery. Robert and Margaret Johnson are the proprietors of Webster Manor and have 25 comfortable rooms for guests. All but two have private baths. The house and guest rooms are attractively furnished in antiques. Coffee or tea is complimentary; breakfasts are served on request for an extra fee. Parking is available at the house, and there are restaurants close by.

Webster Manor, 115 E. James Street, Mullins, SC 29574; (803) 464-9632. (Located half a block off North Main Street in front of the post office.) Rates: $45 per week single; $55 per week double. Cash or personal checks accepted. And to quote Mrs. Johnson: "Only house-trained dogs and children welcome." Open year-around.

Charleston

If your antennae are at all sensitive, you may note a certain air of gentle condescension towards strangers in Charleston. It is not that Charlestonians are intolerant of visitors; on the contrary, they are extremely gracious, courtly mannered folk who want outsiders to come and appreciate their lovely old city as much as they do. That nebulous air of superiority you perceive is inherited. For Charleston, way back in the 1600s, was established and then governed for a time by the only true aristocracy in American history.

The Lords Proprietors who first ruled the Carolinas set up a feudal system of government complete with four houses of parliament and three orders of nobility. Charleston was founded by Anthony Ashley Cooper, Earl of Shaftesbury, and the city's aristocratic tradition began with its first leaders — the dukes, barons and earls who owned the area's vast rice and indigo plantations.

The idea of a New World British-style nobility did not set too well in the Carolinas, however (certainly not with the masses of ordinary colonists who came here primarily to get away from that sort of thing). The era of the ruling class lasted less than half a century. But in Charleston, the Ghosts of Nobility Past still lurk in the narrow cobblestone streets and in the old houses behind their lacy wrought-iron gates. Their spirit is still quite discernible in the patrician attitude of native Charlestonians. Actually, it's nice — a rather genial form of *noblesse oblige* towards those of us unfortunate enough not to be Charleston born and bred.

Charleston has been called "the most civilized town in the world." It is unquestionably a durable one, for it has survived two wars, fire and even earthquake. It is also one of the best preserved communities in America. After the Civil War, when the disappearance of slave labor brought the day of the great plantations to a close, Charleston fell upon hard times. Over the years the historic old houses and other structures fell into disrepair, and it has only been in recent years that renovation has been possible. Once a common saying in Charleston was: "too poor to paint, too proud to whitewash." Today, a great many of the city's handsome buildings have been restored to their original appearance.

Charleston is a delightful city for walking. Its streets are shaded by great live oaks adrip with Spanish moss; the air is fragrant with the scents of jasmine, honeysuckle, magnolia and mimosa. History is everywhere. A marked walking tour, the History Trail, will lead you from White Point Gardens (the Battery) past a long list of historic eighteenth- and nineteenth-century houses, museums and churches. Uniquely Charleston is Rainbow Row, its 14 narrow homes all painted in different colors. Pay a visit to Dock Street Theatre, built in 1736 as the first structure in America to be used solely for theatrical purposes. The present building is a faithful reconstruction, and productions of many sorts are still presented there.

Take a stroll around the grounds of the Citadel, too, the Military College of South Carolina. On Fridays during the school year visitors can watch the cadets performing colorful precision drills on dress parade. A harbor boat tour will take you out to historic Fort Sumter, where the first shots were exchanged between the Union and the Confederacy. If you are traveling with children, do not miss Charles Towne Landing, a new addition to the city. This unusual park was created on the site of the original 1670 settlement and has reconstructed fortifications, a Colonial Village with a seventeenth-century crop garden, nature trails, an ultramodern pavilion and an animal forest where creatures that would have been common in the seventeenth century roam freely.

If you're not a walker, another pleasant way to see Charleston is to take a tour by horse or mule-drawn carriage. Narrated bus tours are also available, or you can rent a bike and set off on your own. Details on all tours and walks may be acquired at the Visitor Information Center at 85 Calhoun Street.

For a glimpse of how those long-ago planters lived, drive out to Boone Hall Plantation, eight miles north of the city. Dating back to 1681, Boone Hall was primarily a cotton plantation and covered 17,000 acres. Ancient moss-draped live oaks line the ¾-mile entrance drive; the original cotton gin house and nine slave houses are still standing. And there is Drayton Hall, nine miles northwest of Charleston. The immense two-story mansion, built in 1738, is a superb example of Georgian Palladian architecture.

No visitor to Charleston could possibly leave without a trip to one or more of its splendid gardens. Magnolia Plantation and Gardens, located ten miles north, dates back to the late 1600s. Today the 30 acres of gardens offer a glorious springtime display of camellias, magnolias, a profusion of azaleas and hundreds of other kinds of flowers. The plantation is the ancestral home of the Draytons and has been in the same family since 1671. The house is open for tours, and there is a petting zoo on the grounds, a miniature-horse ranch and a 150-acre wildlife refuge through which visitors can take a canoe or boat ride.

Middleton Place Gardens, oldest landscaped gardens in America, were started in 1741. They are located 15 miles northwest of Charleston. On the grounds are the house, a Tudor mansion built in 1755, and stableyards, both open to the public. The gardens rise from the river in sweeping terraces; paired butterfly lakes lie at their foot. In addition to its flowers, Middleton also offers a raft of festivals throughout the year: a Greek Spring Festival in May, Arthur Middleton's Birthday Celebration in June; Scottish Highland Games in September, a medieval Lancing Tournament in October and, in November, the harvest-time Plantation Days.

Cypress Gardens is a bit further out, 24 miles north of the city. It is a seductively peaceful place, 160 acres of water gardens with giant cypresses, azaleas and sub-tropical flowers. You can take a boat trip through the lagoons; the craft floats, lazily, silently over black waters that reflect the stately trees and lovely flowers. The gardens were originally a wild, native cypress forest, which hid the famed "Swamp Fox," General Francis Marion, during the Revolutionary War.

The best time to visit the Charleston gardens is in the spring, when the azaleas and other flowers are in full bloom. Cypress Gardens are open only from February 15 to May 1. Magnolia Plantation and Middleton Place Gardens are open year-around.

In late May and early June, Charleston presents the internationally acclaimed Spoleto Festival, U.S.A. The festival was founded in Spoleto, Italy, by the renowned composer-conductor Gian Carlo Menotti and offers a wonderfully comprehensive program of opera, ballet, modern dance, jazz, drama and symphonic, choral and chamber music. Each spring and again in the fall, Charleston opens many of its finest private homes to the public for an assortment of home and garden tours, some of them by romantic candlelight. The rest of the year visitors can only peer wistfully at most of them from the outside.

There are, however, several historic buildings in which you are invited to stay as a welcome guest! Some are houses dating back to the eighteenth and nineteenth centuries; two, now renovated and remodeled, were once old warehouses. Each one allows travelers to share in the special quality of Charleston, past and present. All provide the unique Charleston brand of gracious Southern hospitality.

Sweet Grass Inn. The latest of Charleston's old structures to become a guest house, the Sweet Grass Inn was originally a warehouse. Located in the most historical section of the city, the building was constructed in the late 1700s or early 1800s to serve Charleston's flourishing seaport. The area was once known as the "French Quarter," and several of its streets and alleys have distinctively French names.

The transformation from old warehouse to new guest house came about in an interesting way. In recent years as Charleston became more and more of an attraction for tourists, especially during the Spoleto Festival, the Chamber of Commerce began asking citizens who were so inclined to open their homes to guests during the peak season. Joye Meares Craven did this for one spring and enjoyed it so thoroughly that she decided to make it a full-time venture.

After much planning, she purchased a building in the heart of Old Charleston and proceeded to renovate it. Great care was taken to preserve as many of the finely crafted details as possible. The venerable three-story structure was put together with mortising and pegs; no nails were used. Some of the pegs are still visible, and the floors are random-width heart pine planks, some of them fourteen inches wide. The newly remodeled Sweet Grass Inn opened its doors to guests in September 1980.

There are nine double guest rooms; two of them include sitting rooms that can be converted to accommodate extra people. Six of the rooms have queen-size beds; two have a double bed and a single; and one has a double bed plus a sleeper sofa in the living room. All have private baths, and each guest room is totally different in design and furnishings.

The pleasant roof-terrace added during the restoration offers an unobstructed panoramic view of the harbor, including Fort Sumter. It's a delightfully inviting place where guests may sun, relax in the evening breezes or enjoy their breakfast and morning paper. Breakfast (coffee, juice, fruit, cheese, and special breads) and the newspaper are included in the rates. Joye Craven also keeps each room supplied with fruit and candy.

There is a parlor for guests to use, too, and on wintery nights a cozy fire blazes away in the fireplace. Mrs. Craven states that the emphasis at Sweet Grass Inn is on quaintness, warmth and comfort.

Three fine restaurants are less than a quarter of a block away; others are within easy walking distance. Also nearby are the old Charleston Market, several historic churches, intriguing antique shops and numerous other places of interest. Four excellent beaches are only 15 to 30 minutes away.

Sweet Grass Inn, 23 Vendue Range, Charleston, SC 29401; (803) 723-9980. (Off of East Bay Street.) Single $48; double without sitting room $55; double with sitting room $75; three people in room $62. Cash and personal checks accepted; no credit cards. No pets, please, and no young children. Open year-around.

The Hayne House. Mr. and Mrs. Benjamin C. Chapman are your hosts in the exceptionally attractive Hayne House. Built in 1755 with an 1890 Victorian addition, the house remained in the Hayne family for many years. When the Chapmans moved in, in 1977, they decided it would be fun—as well as a good way to finance the restoration—to have guests stay in the extra bedrooms. Ann Chapman says: "We've found it to be delightful, and a great way to meet people from all over, many of whom have become our friends."

The Chapmans' guests have a choice of either a second-floor suite or a large dormer room on the third floor. The suite offers spacious, airy rooms complete with a fireplace, an antique four-poster bed, lots of good books for reading and a private bath, with steam. There is also a day bed for an additional person. The dormer, also with private bath, is furnished with French

The Hayne House, Charleston, S.C.

twin beds, a gate-legged table, Sheraton mirror and other lovely pieces; it, too, is well-supplied with books. Both accommodations are air conditioned and have television. Complimentary coffee and tea are provided, and on-street parking is available.

The Hayne House is right in the center of the historic area of Charleston; the harbor and Battery are only two blocks away. The warm and friendly Chapmans will be delighted to give directions to Charleston's other points of interest and suggest some good shops and restaurants.

The Hayne House, 30 King Street, Charleston, SC 29401; (803) 577-2633. Second-floor suite: single $40, double $45. Third-floor accommodations: single $30, double $35. Extra person in either, $6. Cash, personal and traveler's checks accepted. No pets, please. Open year-around.

Vendue Inn. If you've ever longed to turn back the pages of time and return to another, gentler, era, you will love the Vendue Inn. Its owners, Evelyn and Morton Needle, have transformed a 181-year-old warehouse into one of Charleston's most appealing guest houses, offering an atmosphere of eighteenth-century elegance and quiet charm.

In the lobby, nicely appointed with antiques, a portrait of An-

GUEST HOUSES

drew Jackson greets guests. Nearby, there is a cool, secluded indoor courtyard with flowers, hanging pots of greenery and an airy spiral staircase. You're invited to take morning coffee here or join the other guests for afternoon wine and cheese. Sometimes the wine sipping will be accompanied by a concert of chamber music performed by local musicians, and during the Spoleto Festival, tea is served in the brick-walled courtyard every afternoon.

The 18 individually decorated guest rooms (all with private baths, air conditioning and color television) feature a cannon ball, brass or canopy bed, quilted bedspreads, brass lamps on Queen Anne and Chippendale tables, Audubon prints, oil paintings and lithographs. The old pine floors are enhanced by the glowing tones of Oriental rugs; the bedspreads, draperies and wallpaper in each room were chosen by Mrs. Needle to complement the colors of the rugs.

The rooms are all named for prominent eighteenth-century South Carolinians; their names (rather than numbers) are placed on the doors and a biographical sketch is inside the room. Visitors are invited to see each available room and then to choose the one they like best. At night maids turn down the beds and place a foil-wrapped chocolate on each pillow. After 10 p.m., security guards watch over the house.

Vendue Inn, bounded on one side by the original cobblestone street, is located in the historical district within walking distance of smart specialty shops, unique antique shops, fine restaurants and a wealth of historic sites. Parking is provided, and a complimentary Continental breakfast is not only available, but is brought to you in your room by a butler!

The Needles also own a recently acquired second guest facility, a beautifully restored town mansion dating back to 1814. It is called *Vendue House* and is primarily for the use of longer staying guests. A number of suites surround a lovely Charleston courtyard and a magnificent marble staircase leads up to the main entrance. The high-ceilinged rooms with their exquisite old moldings offer a taste of long-ago Charleston. One of the suites (adjoining a piazza) features a drawing room with an Adams mantel and a handsome cypress room with king-size rice-canopied bed.

Vendue Inn, 19 Vendue Range, Charleston, SC 29401; (803) 577-7970. (Off East Bay Street near the waterfront.) Doubles $63 and $67; single $58. Vendue House: rates depend on length of stay; please in-

quire. Major credit cards, personal checks and cash are accepted. No pets, please. Open year-around.

Vendue Inn, Charleston, S.C.

The Battery Carriage House. In 1845, Samuel N. Stevens built a house at 20 South Battery Street in Charleston, overlooking the harbor and the Battery. Twenty-five years later Colonel Richard Lathers purchased the place and set about turning the original, simpler residence into an architectural fashion plate of the period. Lathers, a retired millionaire, had returned to the South to help rebuild the state after the Civil War. He hoped that his house would serve "as a meeting place for men of good will, from both the North and the South."

And so it did. The Charleston *News and Courier* reported on a gala evening at the mansion in April 1873 — a party given in honor of Horatio Seymour, ex-governor of New York, and William Cullen Bryant, editor of the *New York Evening Post.* It was described as "one of the most notable social events of the Charleston season," gathering "a most select and fashionable assemblage, including the most prominent gentlemen of the city, with their ladies, as well as a number of military guests from the garrison at the Citadel."

Today, the mansion is the home of Frank and Becky Gay, and

its elegant ambiance may be shared by guests of good will from everywhere. The rooms available for guests are located on the ground floor and in the beautifully restored separate carriage house. They are all furnished in eighteenth-century style, with wide, canopied beds, Oriental rugs and historic Charleston wallpapers and fabrics. All include phone, color television, stereo, radio, a fully equipped kitchenette and a concealed wet bar. The last is stocked with soft drinks and a complimentary bottle of wine, replenished daily. The rooms are air conditioned, and all have private baths.

The rates include a Continental breakfast of coffee, juice and either English muffins laden with strawberry jam or the famous Benedict cheesecake made from a treasured family recipe. Breakfast is served in your room or in the garden between 7:30 and 10 a.m. The brick-walled garden, with its wisteria arbor, potted plants and Battery benches, is a delightful place at any time of the day or evening. Mr. and Mrs. Gay will most likely be on hand in late afternoon, pouring a glass of sherry for their guests. There is also a small, heated swimming pool for visitors' enjoyment.

The house, with its broad piazzas, sits behind handsome wrought-iron gates overlooking the Battery and harbor. It is close to a wealth of appealing shops, good restaurants, historic houses and churches. And the Gays provide bicycles for guests' use, if you'd like to set off on a pedaling tour of Charleston.
The Battery Carriage House, 20 South Battery, Charleston, SC 29401; (803) 723-9881. Single accommodations $44-$48; double $53-$63. Major credit cards are accepted. Open year-around.

Sword Gate Inn. David and Suzanne Redd are the owners of Sword Gate, another of Charleston's magnificent eighteenth-century mansions and one of the most illustrious. During its long history, the house has served as a girl's seminary and as the British Consulate. George Hopley, the British Consul in 1849, added the famous sword gates for which the house is named. A superb example of wrought-iron art, the gates are designed with two spears joined at the center of a broadsword to form a cross. Hopley also installed the gilded mirrors in the antique-filled second-floor ballroom, which guests are invited to tour.

The Sword Gate Inn also has, it is said, a resident ghost. She was the owner of the girls' school, and her name (in case you should chance to run into her) is Madame Talvande.

The mansion fronts on Legare (pronounced "Legree") Street, but the entrance to the Inn is on Tradd Street, through a cobbled brick courtyard. Parking is available. Four rooms for guests are located on the ground floor. Each has its own tile bath, sitting area, double and twin bed, color television, private phone and air conditioning, and the Redds place fresh fruit and flowers in the rooms. Each room is decorated differently with comfortable furniture, including some antiques such as four-poster and brass beds. The ground floor rooms all open directly onto the courtyard. In addition, there is a large upstairs room—at the very top of the house—with a grand view of the city. It has its own private bath and is furnished with a four-poster canopy bed and a nice selection of other period pieces.

David Redd, a native Charlestonian, is the choirmaster and organist at Charleston's historic First Baptist Church and organist and carilloneur at the Citadel. All of the Redds, including Martha Sue, age 15, and David, Jr., age 11, work together as a family to assure the comfort of their guests. They will be delighted to make arrangements for a private history tour of the city, and there are bicycles available for guests, for touring on their own.

The rates include the morning newspaper (brought to the door) and a generous Charleston breakfast served in the mansion's old kitchen near the enormous walk-in brick hearth or out on the flower-bedecked porch. The menu varies, but might include grits or sausage and hash-browned potatoes, stewed cinnamon apples, English muffins and strawberry jam or sweet rolls, juice and coffee. In addition, guests may help themselves to coffee, tea and ice at all hours.

Sword Gate Inn, 111 Tradd Street, Charleston, SC 29401; (803) 723-8518. (From I-26 take Meeting Street Exit, turn right on Broad Street, left on Legare, left on Tradd—Sword Gate is the second driveway on the right. From 17 South, use right lane as your cross the Ashley River and stay right onto Lockwood Blvd. which curves onto Broad Street; turn right on Legare, left on Tradd. From 17 North, use right lane as you cross Cooper River Bridge and take exit marked Meeting Street South/Downtown; drive south on Meeting, turn right on Broad, left on Legare and left on Tradd. Single $48; double $52; third person in room $10 extra. Cash and personal checks only. No pets and no young children, please. Open year-around.

Two Meeting Street. The grand old house at Two Meeting

GUEST HOUSES

Street has an interesting history. A banker named George Walton Williams purchased the lot in 1890 and had the 17-room Queen Anne-style mansion built to his specifications. These included slate roofs with massive turrets and towers, enormous porches, high ceilings and windows and 12-foot sliding doors made of carved oak. Then he added stained glass windows by Tiffany, seventeenth-century Dutch fireplace tiles and imported marble baths. The house took two years to build. Williams gave the place to his daughter for a wedding present when she married into a prestigious old British family, the Carringtons. Not to be outdone, the Carringtons gave the young couple a two-year tour of Europe!

The mansion was used as a private residence until 1944, when Mrs. J. H. Carr and her husband purchased it as their retirement home and decided to open a portion of it to guests. Mrs. Carr, now widowed, and her sister keep the first floor of the house for their personal use; guest accommodations are on the second and third floors. Visitors from June to October will be greeted at Two Meeting Street by the delightful Mr. Donald Wells. The rest of the year Mr. Victor Devlet, another charming gentleman, acts as host.

Mr. Wells' mother, Susan Bradford Wells, was a Massachusetts native, a descendant of Governor William Bradford. Mr. Wells has lived at Two Meeting Street for 13 years, in service to Mrs. Carr and her family. Mr. Devlet is a retired New York stockbroker who spends his summers in Canada.

Downstairs at Two Meeting Street there is a large reception hall with a desk for checking in and out. Guests are given a front door key so they may come and go as they please. In summer guests may rock to their heart's content on the porches, which face the harbor and White Point Gardens (the Battery). House rules are simple: enjoy yourself, but be as quiet as you can so as not to disturb the other guests. (No guest is bothered by loud televisions or radios—there are none.)

From June through October, rooms on the second floor only are available. Room Number One has a private bath; Rooms Number Two and Number Three (reserved for family groups) share a bath and accommodate eight persons. Room Number Four (the oval-gold room), also for family groups, accommodates five or six persons and has its own private bath. Room Number Five has a private bath, twin beds, and its own balcony overlooking the Park. All of the rooms are cooled by electric fans. In the hallway there is a refrigerator for guests' use.

From September through early June, rooms on the third floor are also available. (These rooms would be too warm for comfort in the summer.) The four third-floor rooms each accommodate two persons; two baths are shared, and there is a refrigerator in the hall.

Two Meeting Street, Charleston, SC 29401; (803) 723-7322. Second-floor rooms $20 per day for one or two persons in room, plus $5 extra for each additional adult or child. Third-floor rooms $15 per day for one or two persons. (Note: these rates will most likely be increased somewhat in the near future, so please ask.) Cash or personal checks accepted. No pets or alcoholic beverages are allowed. Check-in times are between 9 a.m. and 8 p.m. only, no later. Open year-around.

Tennessee

One of Tennessee's proudest claims is that no matter where you are, there is a state or national park within an hour's drive. The topography of this diverse state ranges from fertile Delta plains along the Mississippi River in the west to rugged, ancient mountains in the east. More than half of Tennessee's land is forested.

For travelers who enjoy outdoor activities, Tennessee offers just about everything under the sun: excellent fishing, hunting, boating, skiing, camping, canoeing and hiking. Speleologists may be interested to know that the state has more than 2500 caves. For the less physically inclined, the state offers a wealth of other attractions: great scenic beauty, historical sites galore, exciting cities to explore and, throughout the year, a host of festivals.

Two hundred years ago, Tennessee was our nation's western-most frontier. Hernando de Soto roamed around the Mississippi Valley region much earlier—back in the mid-1500s. But Tennessee did not really get moving until the 1700s when it was part of the vast North Carolina Territory. In the latter part of the eighteenth century, many intrepid souls journeyed west over the mountains from the Carolinas and Virginia in search of new land to settle.

Daniel Boone made his way from North Carolina, passed through Tennessee, then went on to Kentucky. Andrew Jackson, too, came from North Carolina, but he stayed in Tennessee and later served as U.S. Congressman and Senator, as a judge and major general, and finally as the seventh President of the United States. Sam Houston, from Virginia, moved to Tennessee as a boy. Houston ran away from home to live with the Cherokees; as an adult he served in Congress, then became governor of Tennessee. Three months after his marriage, however, he resigned the governorship, left his wife and re-joined the Indians for a time before finally settling in Texas. Davy Crockett, yet another legendary American hero, was born in Tennessee; he also ended up in Texas—at the Alamo, where he died.

The first settlements in the Tennessee region were established in the east, near the mountains. The land was believed to be Virginia territory, but actually belonged to North Carolina. North Carolina refused to protect the settlements from Indian attacks; instead, it handed over the entire outlying territory to the federal government. The indignant settlers retaliated by forming their own independent State of Franklin. But Congress refused to recognize it as a State of the Union, and North Carolina took possession once more. In 1790 North Carolina ceded the territory to the U.S. Government once again, and in 1796 Tennessee joined the Union as its sixteenth state.

During the Civil War, Tennessee saw more fighting than any other state except Virginia. Four National Military Parks have been established on the sites of the bloody battles of Chickamauga and Chattanooga, Fort Donelson, Shiloh and Stones River. In the twentieth century, the state's economic welfare was given a giant boost through the formation of the Tennessee Valley Authority—a massive federal flood control, electrical power and navigation project.

The bill creating the TVA was adopted by Congress and signed by President Franklin D. Roosevelt in May 1933. From the first, despite claims by private industry that the act was socialistic and unconstitutional, the authority proved enormously successful. A series of stair-step dams along the Tennessee River and its tributaries has controlled the once-frequent flooding and resulting land erosion. Navigation has been facilitated, and a vast amount of inexpensive electrical power has been generated; in addition, the numerous lakes formed by TVA dams now offer some of the best recreational fishing and boating in the country.

WEST TENNESSEE

We will begin a brief exploration of the state at Memphis, down at the southwestern corner of Tennessee. The state's largest city, Memphis is a thriving, modern river port with a touch of the Old South. You can take a ride on the Mississippi on a riverboat, wander through the superb Overton Park Zoo or enjoy the 88-acre Memphis Botanic Garden. Victorian Village offers a marvelous concentration of nineteenth-century architecture and nine historic churches. There is Libertyland, a new family theme park, and Chucalissa, a fascinating archaeological site where an ancient Indian temple and several native houses have been uncovered and reconstructed. Graceland, Elvis Presley's mansion, is located in Memphis, too, but the grounds are not open to the public.

MIDDLE TENNESSEE

Nashville, capital of Tennessee, lies approximately in the center of the state. It is an old city, first settled in 1779 as Fort Nashborough. President Andrew Jackson's beautiful home, The Hermitage, is open to visitors; Jackson and his wife are buried in the garden. Another of the city's famous structures is The Parthenon, a replica of the original temple in Athens, Greece. It was built for the 1897 Tennessee Centennial and to-day contains a collection of pre-Columbian artifacts, replicas of the Elgin Marbles and art works from the nineteenth and twentieth centuries.

The famed Natchez Trace, an ancient Indian trail that became the most heavily traveled road in the Old Southwest in the 1800s, once ended at Nashville. Someday the scenic parkway that more or less follows the trace's original course will be completed all the way from Natchez, Mississippi to Nashville. Currently, however, it ends at Gordonsburg, Tennessee. Belle Meade, a gracious plantation house just outside of Nashville, was once a way station on the trace.

Historic though it is, Nashville's major claim to fame is its music. It calls itself "Music City U.S.A.," and with good reason. Two centuries ago Nashville's early settlers brought with them the mountain music of their homes back east in the Smokies. The "hillbilly" music grew and became the Grand Ole Opry, then the "Nashville Sound," a mixture of country and western. And Nashville grew into one of the world's largest recording centers. Opryland U.S.A., a 110-acre musical theme park, tells the story of American music from folk to jazz. It is the site of the new Grand Ole Opry House and offers more than seventy musical productions daily, ranging from classic country to a futuristic sound and light show with rock and disco.

Stones River National Battlefield is located near Murfreesboro, southeast of Nashville, and Shiloh National Military Park is just west of Waynesboro, to the southwest.

EAST TENNESSEE

Tennessee's eastern border is mountainous. Down in the southeast are Chattanooga and Lookout Mountain. Nearby is the nation's oldest and largest military park, Chickamauga and

GUEST HOUSES

Chattanooga National Park. It begins nine miles south of Chattanooga and extends into neighboring Georgia. Continuing on to the northeast, you will come to Gatlinburg, starting point for the Great Smoky Mountains National Park.

Gatlinburg may once have been a quaint little mountain hamlet, but today—despite its spectacular setting in a valley surrounded by forested peaks—it is a crowded conglomeration of tourist enterprises. Amidst all the inevitable tacky souvenirs, however, are scores of excellent craft shops and studios offering some of the region's finest handmade items—quilts, wooden toys and games, split-oak baskets, dulcimers and other musical instruments and attractive handwoven materials.

Knoxville, northwest of Gatlinburg, is the home of the University of Tennessee and the headquarters of the Tennessee Valley Authority. There are six TVA lakes within 30 miles, and the Great Smoky Mountains National Park is 39 miles away. Oak Ridge, "the atomic city" built during World War II by the U.S. Government, is just a few miles west of Knoxville. The American Museum of Science and Energy contains some fascinating exhibits describing the roles of nuclear and other forms of energy in health, power, agriculture, industry and research. Visitors may also examine the famed 1943 Graphite Reactor at the Oak Ridge National Laboratory.

The state of Tennessee, abounding as it is in outdoor sports, historical and cultural activities, country-western music and fabulous scenery, lacks but one thing—a selection of guest houses. There are a few scattered here and there, but we have been able to include only one in this book. (As we mentioned in the Introduction, we would be delighted to hear about any others you may chance to discover on your travels.) The lone Tennessee guest house is located in Rogersville, a small town near the Holston River in the northeast portion of the state, one and a half hours from the Smokies. The Holston River offers great fishing; the country club has a fine golf course; and several of the beautiful TVA lakes are close by for swimming and boating.

Kyle House. Kyle House is a large, three-story brick Georgian, with high ceilings and well-proportioned rooms. Mrs. Kay Kyle owns the historic old house, built around 1830 by slaves; all the bricks are handmade. In the mid-1800s, Mrs. Kyle relates, a good part of the town was encompassed in the building: The Bank of Rogersville, law offices and a hotel. During the Civil

War the house was used as Confederate headquarters.

The Kyle family has owned the place for more than a hundred years, and the house is completely furnished with antiques, all inherited from the Kyle and Boone (maternal grandparents) families. Kyle House sits on an acre and a half of beautifully landscaped gardens, and guests are most welcome to wander around and enjoy them.

Kay Kyle has four comfortable, attractively decorated rooms for guests: two singles and two doubles, sharing two baths. The rates are amazingly reasonable, only $4.50 for single occupancy and $8.00 for double! No meals are served, but your hostess will be delighted to suggest some good places to eat in town. Parking is available at the house.

Kyle House, 111 W. Main Street, Rogersville, TN 37857; (615) 272-8960. (Located in downtown Rogersville, on Business Rte. 11W, diagonally across from the Court House.) Single $4.50 per night; double $8. Cash or personal checks accepted. Pets and children are welcome. Open year-around.

Virginia and Washington, D.C.

History is everywhere (and irresistible) in the Old Dominion State of Virginia. There is scarcely an inch of ground that does not tell a story—from America's seventeenth-century beginnings at Jamestown and the pre-revolutionary capital of Williamsburg to Civil War battlefields and Appomatox Court House where that bloody struggle came to an end. The state abounds in historic sites and buildings, including a host of stately plantation homes where visitors are offered a fascinating glimpse into Virginia's aristocratic past. Virginia is a stunningly beautiful state, a diverse land stretching from the Tidewater region, Eastern Shore and beaches to ancient mountain highlands and the lovely Shenandoah Valley.

In 1584 Sir Walter Raleigh sent a small band of English explorers to investigate the region. The expedition named it *Virginia* for Elizabeth, England's Virgin Queen. But it was not until 1607 that Virginia's real history—and that of our nation—began. In May of that year the first permanent English colony in America was founded here on the banks of the James River. The settlement was established by the London Company under a grant from King James I and was named (as was the river) for him.

The Jamestown colony, which started out with 104 persons, was reduced to about 60 during the following three years; the rest were victims of Indian attacks, illness and famine. In 1610, however, more colonists and supplies arrived, and life in the settlement took a turn for the better. John Rolfe assured the colony's future by establishing the tobacco-growing industry. He also improved relations between the colonists and the Indians by marrying Pocahontas, daughter of the great Indian chief, Powhatan.

The king revoked Virginia's charter in 1624 and made it a royal colony, ruled directly by the crown through a royal governor. Although the colony was now prosperous and growing rapidly in population, its citizens began to resent England's imposition of burdensome taxes, as well as other high-handed acts. Also, the Indians were once again hostile, attacking outlying settlers in a series of savage raids. Governor William Berkeley refused to send help, and in 1676 a planter named Nathaniel Bacon formed an army of colonists and marched on the Indians, defeating them soundly. Governor Berkeley, instead of being grateful for the intervention, proclaimed Bacon to be a "rebel." Feeling that Jamestown was the seat of British oppression, Bacon then marched on the capital, twice, burning it on his second visit. Shortly thereafter he died of malaria and his "rebellion" (a forerunner of the American Revolution) collapsed.

In the period before the Revolution, however, Virginia (then the largest of the colonies) led the other colonies in resistance to the crown. Her royal governor was driven out in 1775, and a raft of Virginians including George Washington, Patrick Henry and Thomas Jefferson became revolutionary leaders. In 1778 Virginia became the tenth state to join the Union.

Before the Civil War, almost a century later, the state opposed secession at first and changed its stance only when President Lincoln sent out his call for troops. Robert E. Lee, a Virginian, resigned his commission in the U.S. Army to become commander-in-chief of the Confederate forces, and during the war the state was one of the major battlegrounds of the Confederacy.

Virginia was readmitted to the Union in 1870. After surviving the difficult Reconstruction years, it went on to become one of the South's most progressive states. Its tobacco industry is still thriving today, along with other forms of agriculture; its seaports, with their superb natural harbors, still support an important commercial shipping and shipbuilding industry. Tourism in Virginia is big business, too. The state offers vacationers year-around seashore and mountain recreation, including all manner of sports activities, and an almost limitless choice of historic and scenic attractions.

NORTHEASTERN VIRGINIA
AND WASHINGTON, D.C.

Most visitors to Washington, D.C., want to see our nation's capital *and* the wealth of historic sites in neighboring northeastern Virginia. Separated only by the Potomic River, the two share much of the same history—part of the original District of Columbia once belonged to Virginia.

Washington is a beautiful city of wide, tree-lined streets, imposing government buildings and a fascinating collection of museums. Major Pierre Charles L'Enfant designed the city in 1791, working under the supervision of President George Washington. L'Enfant's plan for the new capital is still considered remarkable today—a gridiron pattern of north and south streets, diagonal avenues and the magnificent park called the Mall, with the Capitol Building as the focal point.

Wonderful though it is to see, however, Washington is not a joy for motorists. L'Enfant's design was not meant for twentieth-century automobile traffic; even the residents find the streets confusing to negotiate in a car, and parking is a real problem. The easiest way to get around is via the excellent new subway system, the Metro. Or, take one of the many sightseeing tours available. A good place to begin exploring is the National Visitor Center on Massachusetts Avenue at First Street, N.E., in the restored Union Station Building. Knowledgeable personnel will supply information and brochures and help organize your stay. The center is open 8 a.m. to 8 p.m. daily from March to November; to 6 p.m. December to February; closed on Christmas.

The following are some of Washington's most-visited sites:

The U.S. Capitol, Capitol Hill. Construction began on the Capitol in 1793, but the building was not finished until 1867. During those years it was enlarged a number of times, and after the British burned it in 1814, it was completely rebuilt. In 1962 a further expansion took place. The Senate meets in one wing, the House of Representatives in the other. The Capitol is open to visitors from 9 a.m. to 4:30 p.m. daily except for Thanksgiving, Christmas and New Year's Day.

The U.S. Supreme Court. Just behind the Capitol, the Supreme Court Building was completed in 1935. The impressive courtroom is open to the public except for holidays; there are interpretive tours from 9:30 a.m. to 5 p.m. Monday through Friday.

Library of Congress. Located next to the Supreme Court Building, the Library of Congress was established in 1800. The British burned it, too, during the War of 1812, and it had to be started all over again. Thomas Jefferson aided the cause by contributing about 6500 volumes from his own collection. Today the library houses some 73 million books, manuscripts, recordings, maps and prints, photographs and other materials, including such priceless treasures as a Gutenberg Bible. The exhibit halls are open Monday through Friday from 8:30 a.m. to 6 p.m. Guided tours are available weekdays from 9 a.m. to 8 p.m. weekends and holidays from 9 a.m. to 5 p.m.

Folger Shakespeare Library. One of the world's finest collections of Shakespearean and English Renaissance books is contained in the Folger Shakespeare Library, behind the Library of Congress. It is open 10 a.m. to 4:30 p.m. daily; closed Sundays and holidays.

Museum of African Art. The Museum of African Art is housed in the one-time home of Frederick Douglass, the famed nineteenth-century black abolitionist, orator and publisher. On view are brilliantly hued textiles, musical instruments and hundreds of works of sculpture that represent more than 60 African tribal styles. Live performances of music and dance are regularly offered, plus craft exhibitions and films. There is also an excellent gift shop with an array of unusual items. It is open 11 a.m. to 5 p.m. on weekdays, noon to 5 p.m. on weekends.

The National Archives. The National Archives building is located between Pennsylvania and Constitution Avenues. Here you can see the original Declaration of Independence, the Constitution and Bill of Rights, and other of our nation's most historic documents. It is open Monday through Saturday 9 a.m. to 6 p.m., 1 p.m. to 6 p.m. on Sundays.

National Gallery of Art. The East and West Buildings of the National Gallery of Art are on Constitution Avenue. Masterpieces galore fill these enormous structures. They hold art treasures from the thirteenth to the twentieth century. Hours are 10 a.m. to 5 p.m. Monday through Saturday, noon to 9 p.m. on Sunday.

Smithsonian Institution. At the Smithsonian (on the Mall), an absolutely incredible number of things, encompassing practically all of human culture, are housed in a group of massive buildings. They include the National Portrait Gallery, the National Collection of Fine Arts (American arts) and several other collections such as the Freer Gallery of Art, Renwick Gallery and the Hirshhorn Museum and Sculpture Garden, the National Museum of Natural History, the National Museum of History and Technology, the National Air & Space Museum (with aeronautical firsts ranging from Lindbergh's *Spirit of St. Louis* to astronaut John Glenn's *Friendship*-7 and other space vehicles), the central Smithsonian Institution building and more. It is open 10 a.m. to 5:30 p.m. daily in winter, 10 a.m. to 9 p.m. in summer.

The White House. The nation's most famous house lies beyond the Ellipse, at 1600 Pennsylvania Avenue. Eleven of its rooms are open for tours from 10 a.m. to noon Tuesday through Friday, 10 a.m. to 1 p.m. on Saturday. In summer you'll need to get there early because the lines are long. The gracious mansion has been the official residence of every American president except George Washington. After being burned by the British in 1814, the house was restored and painted white—thus its name.

The Washington Monument. On the other side of the Ellipse, visitors may climb 898 steps or take the elevator to the top of the Washington Monument. The 555-foot-high obelisk was first opened to the public in 1888; its hours are 9 a.m. to 5 p.m. daily in winter, 8 a.m. to midnight in spring and summer.

The Lincoln Memorial. At the end of the Mall next to the Potomac is the Lincoln Memorial. Washington residents often stop late at night on their way home from a party, just to pay homage to this remarkably moving sculpture. Daniel Chester French, who also created the famous Minuteman Statue in Concord, Massachusetts, sculpted the great marble figure of Lincoln.

Thomas Jefferson Memorial. On the south bank of the Tidal Basin, the classically styled Thomas Jefferson Memorial holds a large bronze statue of Jefferson, third president of the United States. In early April or thereabouts, the hundreds of cherry trees that surround the memorial and the Tidal Basin burst into bloom. The trees were a gift to the city of Washington from the mayor of Tokyo, Japan, in 1912.

Ford's Theatre. In 1865, President Abraham Lincoln was assassinated at Ford's Theatre. The building, at 511 Tenth

Street, N.W., has been authentically restored and includes a Lincoln museum. Theatrical performances are held in the theater throughout the year. The house in which Lincoln died, at 516 Tenth Street, is also open to visitors. Museum and house are open from 9 a.m. to 5 p.m.; the theater closes at 1 p.m. on Thursdays and Saturdays.

Georgetown. Home of Georgetown University, which was established in 1789, Georgetown is a colorful mixture of lovely old houses, steep narrow streets and numerous interesting shops and restaurants. It is adjacent to central Washington, just across Rock Creek to the northwest.

The John F. Kennedy Center for the Performing Arts. The Kennedy Center is at New Hampshire Avenue and F Street, N.W., not far from the Lincoln Memorial. Our national cultural center includes an opera house, concert hall and movie and drama theaters. Guided tours are given from 10 a.m. to 1:15 p.m. daily.

Washington churches. The city's notable churches include the National Shrine of the Immaculate Conception, on Michigan Avenue, N.E., the nation's largest Roman Catholic Church; the Franciscan Monastery (with replicas of such great Christian shrines as the Grotto at Lourdes and the Garden of Gethsemane) at 1400 Quincy Street, N.E.; and Washington National Cathedral, a Gothic-style Episcopal cathedral begun in 1907 and still under construction.

National Zoological Park. The main entrance to the National Zoological Park is on Connecticut Avenue, N.W., the 3000 block. Part of the Smithsonian Institution, the zoo is a must for animal watchers. Among the approximately 2500 creatures on display are such very famous ones as Smoky the Bear and our two giant pandas from China. The birdhouse and outdoor flight enclosure are especially interesting and fun; some of the birds seem to take great delight in zooming right past a visitor's nose. Zoo buildings are open from 9 a.m. to 4:30 p.m. daily.

And these are just the highlights! To really appreciate Washington's vast collection of marvels takes time, so try to plan on staying several days, at least. Fortunately for travelers, there is a fine guest house right in the city itself. It is a perfect place to use as a base while sight-seeing around Washington and the adjacent Virginia countryside.

The Connecticut-Woodley Tourist Home. The house is very conveniently located, one block from the National Zoo and half a block from the Metro (subway) station. Embassy Row, the National Cathedral and the Naval Observatory (home of the vice-president) are also nearby, and Georgetown is just a short distance away. The new Sheraton-Washington Hotel (where the rates are approximately double) is directly across the street.

Mr. Ray Knickel owns the Connecticut-Woodley; Mrs. Jean Liebel is the manager. The large, handsome old house, built in 1909, has twelve attractive, air-conditioned guest rooms—two singles, three doubles and seven triples. The accommodations are being converted so that each will have a private bath. Every room will have its own telephone, too. Guests are invited to use the comfortable sitting and television room, and (wonder of wonders in Washington, D.C.) there is private parking.

No food is served, but the hosts will be happy to suggest some excellent places to eat in the vicinity. Ask them to give directions for reaching Washington's multitude of things to see—among them, beautiful Rock Creek Park beyond the zoo where one can jog, hike, bicycle, ride horseback, picnic or play tennis and golf.

Connecticut-Woodley Tourist Home
Washington, D.C.

GUEST HOUSES

The Connecticut-Woodley Tourist Home, 2647 Woodley Road, N.W., Washington, D.C. 20008; (202) 667-0218. (The house is just off Connecticut Avenue. To reach it, proceed either north or south on Connecticut Avenue to the 2700 block; turn west at the intersection of Connecticut and Woodley, and continue to the first house on the right.) Rates are $22 to $27 for singles, $27 to $32 for doubles, $4 for an extra person, special rates for three or more in a family. Cash or personal checks preferred. No pets, please. Open year-around.

Across the Potomac to Virginia is Arlington National Cemetery. Established in 1864, the 420-acre site contains about 174,000 graves; most of those buried here were members of the U.S. armed forces killed in battle. Among the numerous monuments are the Tomb of the Unknown Soldier (now called the Tomb of the Unknowns), which has a round-the-clock military guard, and the Marine Corps Memorial Iwo Jima Statue, which depicts the 1945 raising of the American flag on Mt. Suribachi. Among the many famous Americans buried at Arlington are President John F. Kennedy and his brother Robert, President William Howard Taft, Admiral Robert E. Peary and generals George C. Marshall and John J. Pershing.

Also on the cemetery grounds is the Custis-Lee Mansion, Arlington House. It is open to the public from 9:30 a.m. to 4:30 p.m. in winter, 9:30 a.m. to 6 p.m. in summer. There is a splendid view of Washington from the columned portico. The Greek Revival house was built in 1817 by George Washington's foster son, George Washington Parke Custis. His daughter married Robert E. Lee, and the Lee family lived here until 1861.

If you're traveling with children, pay a visit to Turkey Run Farm, in McLean. Located a few miles northwest of Arlington National Cemetery, the farm includes a re-created Colonial homestead at which costumed interpreters reenact the day-to-day life of the early settlers. It is a far cry from the gracious existence enjoyed by the citizens of Williamsburg; life on a Colonial farm was a constant struggle for survival, and very primitive. Wolf Trap Farm Park for the Performing Arts is just a bit beyond Turkey Run, in Vienna. During the summer months (and occasionally in winter) opera, ballet, folk dance, symphony and contemporary musical performances are held here in an attractive wooded setting.

It may seem unlikely, but the Potomac River is not at all a peaceful, broad, smooth-flowing stream throughout its length. At Great Falls Park, northwest of Wolf Trap (about 15 miles from Washington), the river is dramatically wild and noisy. A 50-foot waterfall, and many smaller ones, cascade over tumbled masses of rock; the surrounding park offers hiking trails and many excellent picnic areas. A word of warning: do not try to climb out on the rocks; the swift water makes them very slippery and dangerous.

South of Arlington National Cemetery is Alexandria. Its restored Old Town and waterfront area contain more than a thousand historic houses. The Alexandria Tourist Council at 221 King Street provides a walking-tour map and shows visitors a 14-minute film, entitled "Alexandria in Virginia—George Washington's Town." When Washington was only 17 and an apprentice surveyor, he helped lay out and map the town's streets.

Along the walking tour are Carlyle House, built in 1752; a 1792 apothecary shop (now a museum of early pharmacy); the home of General Henry (Lighthorse Harry) Lee, the 1785 Lee-Fendall House; Robert E. Lee's Boyhood Home; Gadsby's Tavern dating to the 1770s (often visited by George Washington); and several churches including Christ Church, which contains family pews that once belonged to Washington and Lee.

Another Alexandria building—not on the tour—is The George Washington Masonic National Memorial; it looms over the city from atop Shooter's Hill, rather like a brooding giant. It is 333 feet high, patterned after the ancient lighthouse in Alexandria, Egypt—and indescribably ugly.

To erase its bulk from your mind, head next for one or more of the magnificent plantations in the area. Woodlawn, seven miles south of Alexandria, was completed in 1805. George Washington gave the land, 2000 acres, to his foster daughter Nellie Custis as a wedding present in 1799. The house is open daily from 9:30 a.m. to 4:30 p.m., except Thanksgiving, Christmas and New Year's Day.

George Washington's own Mount Vernon, a few miles away, is an absolute must, even if you see nothing else in the region. The oldest part of the house was built around 1735 by Washington's father; George brought his bride Martha here in 1759, and they are both buried on the grounds. The mansion, a beautifully proportioned white Colonial, sits high on a bluff overlooking the Potomac. From its columned, two-story piazza there is a glorious view over sweeping lawns down to the river below. Both the house and its flanking outbuildings have been perfectly restored.

GUEST HOUSES

George Washington died in 1799, Martha a few years later. A nephew, Bushrod Washington, inherited the place. But by the 1830s the estate had become unproductive; its buildings were falling into disrepair, and gardens and grounds were neglected. In 1853 an enterprising woman named Ann Pamela Cunningham formed the Mount Vernon Ladies' Association. They purchased the place and over the next quarter century or so managed to return it to its original handsome appearance. During the Civil War years, the house, amazingly, survived; as a sort of neutral zone between the opposing forces, it was respectfully visited on various occasions by both Northern and Southern troops.

Mount Vernon is open from 9 a.m. to 5 p.m., March to September; the rest of the year from 9 a.m. to 4 p.m.

Another elegant plantation home is Gunston Hall, about 19 miles south of Alexandria. George Mason, author of the Fairfax Resolves (which served as the model for the Bill of Rights) lived very comfortably here, surrounded by a collection of exquisite furnishings. The red-brick mansion was built in the late 1750s; its classic boxwood gardens are renowned. Gunston Hall is open daily except Christmas from 9:30 a.m. to 5 p.m.

Civil War history buffs will want to visit Manassas (Bull Run) National Battlefield Park, 26 miles southwest of Washington. Two major Civil War battles were fought here, where more than 23,000 men were killed or wounded. Self-guided tours begin at the Visitor Center, and there is a fine museum with an audiovisual presentation and exhibits.

If you have the time, drive on down to Fredericksburg, approximately 50 miles south of Alexandria. Or, plan to pay it a visit on your way to Williamsburg and Jamestown. The Chamber of Commerce proudly calls Fredericksburg "America's Most Historic City." George Washington went to school here; his sister lived here in a handsome Georgian brick manor house; and his mother is buried in Fredericksburg's old cemetery. Other famous residents have included James Monroe and Commodore John Paul Jones.

Fredericksburg—on the Rappahannock River—was a major seagoing port until the 1850s, when the railroads drained off most of its shipping traffic. Then, because of its strategic location between Richmond and Washington, it became a viciously contested prize during the Civil War, changing hands seven times. The four major battles fought in and around the town between 1862 and 1864 left it badly damaged. Somehow, many of its eighteenth-century buildings managed to survive and may be visited today. Walking or driving tours originate at the Bicentennial Visitor Center, a charming 1817 house with a garden courtyard. After viewing a film presentation at the center, wend your way to such historic sites as the Rising Sun Tavern, built around 1760 by George Washington's brother; Kenmore, Washington's sister's home; James Monroe's law office, where he wrote the Monroe Doctrine; Hugh Mercer's Apothecary Shop; and the Old Slave Block.

Fredericksburg and Spotsylvania National Military Park is located just west of the town; the park includes parts of all four of those Civil War battlefields. The engagements—the battles of Fredericksburg, Chancellorsville, Spotsylvania Court House and the Battle of the Wilderness—involved the most concentrated, bloodiest fighting ever to take place on American soil. Miles of automobile roads take visitors on a self-guided tour through much of the park's 5000-acre expanse, past many of the original trenches, the Spotsylvania Court House and the Jackson Shrine, which marks the place where Confederate General "Stonewall" Jackson died. Begin your tour at the National Park Service Visitor Center and Museum, on Old U.S. 1, for information and directions.

VIRGINIA'S TIDEWATER REGION

The Tidewater is Virginia's inner coastal region, a low, flattish area with a ragged shoreline marked by innumerable bays and inlets. The state's great tidal rivers—the Potomac, Rappahannock, York and James—flow through the region into vast Chesapeake Bay. The Bay separates the Tidewater from Virginia's Eastern Shore, a long, narrow peninsula that connects with Maryland to the north. Jamestown, Williamsburg and Yorktown are all located in the Tidewater, as is Virginia Beach, a popular resort area.

Driving down from Washington, D.C., and northeastern Virginia, take I-95 from Fredericksburg to Richmond. (Richmond is a bit west of the Tidewater region, but it's a good place to begin exploration of the area.)

Kings Dominion, about 10 miles north of Richmond (on Va. 30) is an enormous family entertainment complex. Its six theme parks include International Street with a replica of the Eiffel Tower; Old Virginia; Happy Land; Candyapple Grove, a turn-of-the-century amusement park; the Lost World, which offers four fantasy rides enclosed in the world's tallest man-made mountain; and Lion Country Safari, a drive-through wildlife preserve where you may find yourself surrounded by lions, pecked at by ostriches, and halted by elephants crossing the road. (All of these Lion Country adventures happen while you are safely inside your car, windows rolled up.) Kings Dominion is open daily from Memorial Day to late August, on weekends only April to May and late August to October; it is closed the rest of the year.

Richmond, Virginia's capital since 1780 (and the capital of the Confederacy from 1861 to 1865), was first explored by Captain John Smith in 1607. In 1865 fleeing Confederate troops burned bridges, government warehouses and other important structures, starting a conflagration that destroyed a large portion of the city. As in Fredericksburg, some of the oldest buildings were spared. These included the State Capitol, built in 1785; the Governor's Mansion; St. Paul's, St. John's and St. Peter's churches; Robert E. Lee's wartime home; the 1790 John Marshall house; and the Edgar Allen Poe Museum (the house dates back to 1736).

Southeast of Richmond, along the James River, are a number of lovely old plantations. A great many of our early patriots, presidents and other leaders lived in this area. Many of the magnificent houses and their grounds and gardens are open to the public. Va. 5 leads first to Shirley Plantation, about 20 miles from Richmond. Built between 1723 and 1770, it has been the home for nine generations of the Carter family. Berkeley Plantation, built by Benjamin Harrison IV in 1726, is about three miles further. Benjamin Harrison V, signer of the Declaration of Independence, and William Henry Harrison, our ninth president, were born here. Then comes Westover, which was constructed around 1730 by Richmond's founder, William Byrd II, and Sherwood Forest with its 300-foot-long mansion—one of the longest private dwellings in America.

Over on the other side of the river is Brandon Plantation, a 4400-acre estate with much of its land still under cultivation. The gardens are spectacular. Bacon's Castle in Surry County is further along, on Va. 617 off Rte. 10. Built in 1655, the Castle is the last surviving manor house in America constructed in Jacobean style. It was the home of Nathaniel Bacon, that seventeenth-century "rebel" against English rule.

For maps and information about the plantations (of which there are even more than these mentioned), ask at the Metropolitan Richmond Convention & Visitors Bureau, 201 E.

Franklin Street.

Jamestown, Williamsburg and Yorktown

Jamestown, Williamsburg and Yorktown lie to the southeast of Richmond in the area called Virginia's Historic Triangle. The most scenic way to get there is to follow Va. 5 or 10 and 31, past the plantations. For the proper historical perspective, first stop at Jamestown Colonial National Historical Park, on the Colonial Parkway off of Va. 231. It is the site of the first permanent English settlement in America, established in 1607.

Difficulties beset the Jamestown colony from the start: crops failed, the Indians were hostile, and the damp, swampy surroundings fostered malaria and other illnesses. And as if the problem of sheer survival *were* not enough, the colonists bickered constantly among themselves. Captain John Smith, a remarkably able and resourceful man, soon became the group's leader. He pulled the others together after a fashion and organized trade with the Indians, at some risk to himself. Practically everyone knows the romantic story of Smith's being captured by Chief Powhatan and saved from death by Pocahontas, the chief's daughter. (She later married John Rolfe, another Jamestown settler.)

Smith returned to England in October 1609; during the following winter the colony almost went under. The "starving time," as it was called, reduced the inhabitants to about 60 in number. But an influx of new settlers and supplies in 1610 brought new hope, and Jamestown finally began to thrive. The colonists even managed to achieve an impressive number of firsts: they made glass in 1608, began growing tobacco commercially four years later, and in 1619 the first representative assembly in America was held at Jamestown. Jamestown also has the dubious distinction of being the destination of the first black slaves brought to this country from Africa; they arrived here in 1619.

Nathaniel Bacon burned the town in 1676 in revolt against William Berkeley, the royal governor. The Statehouse burned in another fire in 1698, and in 1699 the government moved to nearby Williamsburg. Jamestown was virtually abandoned, and it eventually died out altogether. Today, the only remains of the colony are the foundations of several buildings, an old church tower and traces of streets and boundaries unearthed in archaeological exploration by the National Park Service. The Association for the Preservation of Virginia Antiquities owns about 20 acres of island site; the Park Service and Association together have provided markers and recorded talks that tell Jamestown's story. Stop at the Visitor Center to see exhibits and a film; then walk to the first landing site, the 1620 "New Towne" area, the seventeenth-century church tower and the glasshouse, plus some recently constructed monuments and a 1907 church built on the original foundations.

For a taste of the way life was lived in the 1600s, visit adjacent Jamestown Festival Park. This re-creation of early Jamestown includes John Smith's fort, Powhatan's lodge, thatched cottages and full-scale replicas of the three ships that brought the colonists from England in 1607—the *Susan Constant, Godspeed* and *Discovery*. Exhibits in the Old World (British) and New World (American) pavilions depict the background and chief events of the colony's settlement. The park is closed on Christmas and New Year's Day.

Now follow the Colonial Parkway to Williamsburg, six miles further. The town is situated on a peninsula between the York and James Rivers; it was first settled in 1633 as Middle Plantation, an outpost against Indian attacks. When Virginia's seat of government was moved here from Jamestown in 1699, the town was renamed *Williamsburg* for England's King William III. It was already a college town; the College of William and Mary was founded in 1693. (The college is the second oldest in the country; only Harvard is older.)

Williamsburg quickly became the center of Virginia's political, cultural and social life. The bustling Colonial capital almost boiled over during the twice yearly "publick times" when the legislature met and courts were in session. During those times the town's population doubled; its visitors crowded the inns and taverns and enjoyed a wealth of entertainment: fairs, horse races, banquets and elegant balls.

However, when the capital was removed to Richmond in 1780, Williamsburg's stirring Colonial era came to an end. The old town drowsed on, its historical importance almost forgotten, for a century and a half. During those years many of the original buildings decayed or, even worse, were torn down and replaced by newer structures. Then, in the 1920s, the wealthy philanthropist John D. Rockefeller entered the picture. Inspired by Dr. W. A. R. Goodwin, rector of Bruton Parish Church, Rockefeller financed an awesome undertaking—the restoration of Colonial Williamsburg.

To date, the project (which is not yet quite completed) has

cost close to one hundred million dollars. Architects, historians, landscape gardeners, archaeologists, town planners, builders and many other experts have contributed their talents to the restoration. Their goal has been to recapture not only the physical form, but also the environment of an American eighteenth-century Colonial town.

The restored area (only a small portion of the actual town of Williamsburg) is about one mile long and half a mile wide. Within these boundaries approximately 600 buildings were moved or razed. Some 88 of the original structures have been preserved and restored, and about 50 buildings (among them, the Capitol and Governor's Palace) have been rebuilt upon the original foundations. Gardens have been replanted with care, and authentic furnishings for the houses acquired.

Today Colonial Williamsburg lives again, complete with the sights and sounds (but thankfully, not the smells) of two hundred years ago. "Townsfolk" in typical Colonial attire go about their business—plying their trades, serving meals in the colorful old taverns, driving horse-drawn carriages and wagons or simply stopping to chat awhile with visitors. Guests are invited to wander along the streets, roam through the houses and other buildings with their more than 200 exhibition rooms, enjoy the charming gardens and watch craftspeople at work in their shops. It's a marvelous experience!

Tours begin at the Colonial Williamsburg Information Center, with an introductory 35-minute film. There is even a special tour just for youngsters, and there are evening candlelight tours, too. The Duke of Gloucester Street is the main thoroughfare; the Capitol building where Patrick Henry gave his rousing speech against the Stamp Act is at the east end, the College of William and Mary at the west end. In between are the Raleigh Tavern and Wetherburn's Tavern, the Public Gaol, the handsome Governor's Palace and Gardens, Bruton Parish Church, the Courthouse of 1770, a large number of interesting houses and craft shops and much more. As you roam, you can munch on a freshly baked cooky or spicy gingerbread, or stop for a meal in one of the taverns once patronized by such notables as Thomas Jefferson, Patrick Henry and George Washington.

From mid-March to early October, visitors may watch an exciting militia muster presented twice weekly on Market Square Green or, on Saturdays from April to November, a fife and drum corps parade. Throughout the year all manner of special events take place, including art exhibitions, Colonial fairs and theatrical performances. At Christmastime Williamsburg celebrates the festive season with carols, dancing, candle-lighting ceremonies and fireworks.

The Colonial Parkway next takes you east to Yorktown, on the York River. First settled in the 1630s, the village was official-ly founded in 1691. A thriving seaport up until the mid-1700s, in 1781 Yorktown was the scene of the final action of the American Revolution. The British general Lord Cornwallis and his men were trapped in the town, surrounded by American and French forces under General George Washington. Corn-wallis surrendered after a siege that lasted twenty days. Peace was not officially declared for another two years, but the British defeat brought an end to the war's actual battles. Visitors to Yorktown may explore the battlefield, the Moore House, Swan Tavern and other old buildings.

Carter's Grove, six miles southeast of Williamsburg on U.S. 60, is one of the most beautiful of all the James River planta-tions. The house, built between 1750 and 1753, is open to the public; the pewter collection is especially outstanding. Nearby is a delightful theme park, The Old Country/Busch Gardens. Its 360 acres offer seven re-created Old World hamlets, in-cluding German, English, French and Scottish. Children will love riding on the Loch Ness Monster roller coaster, and there is entertainment of all sorts: puppets, animal acts, magic shows, music, a German "Oktoberfest." The park is closed in winter, open on weekends only from March to June and Labor Day to November, and open daily in summer.

There is so much to do and see in this region of Virginia that you'll probably want to stay several days, if not longer. And Williamsburg provides the ideal base from which to roam. Begin by exploring Colonial Williamsburg itself, then drive over to Jamestown and Yorktown, visit Busch Gardens and the James River plantations or even journey down the coast for a swim at one of the fine beaches about an hour and a half away.

Among the many and varied accommodations in the Williamsburg area are a large number of guest houses. Five of these are described here; for a complete list write to the Williamsburg Chamber of Commerce, P.O. Box HQ, Williamsburg, VA 23185; phone (804) 229-6511. They are all beautifully maintained private homes offering comfortable quarters at very reasonable prices.

"White Oak." White Oak is a charming brick house, built in 1950. Mrs. Arthur B. Strong is hostess, and she has one very attractive guest room with twin beds. Nicely decorated with Colonial-style maple furniture, it includes a pleasant sitting area. The room has its own ground-floor private entrance and bath, telephone and clock-radio, and a fully equipped, built-in modern kitchen. Mrs. Strong usually provides supplies for guests' breakfast on their first morning. Mary Strong says that—if you do not care to cook in—there are scads of excellent restaurants in the vicinity that offer some of the best food in the country! And you can walk from her house to Colonial Williamsburg. On-street parking for your car is available at the house.

White Oak, 129 Indian Springs Road, Williamsburg, VA 23185; (804) 229-1178. (Off Jamestown Road near the College of William and Mary.) Rates: $20 single; $25 double. Cash or personal checks accepted. Open year-round.

White Oak
Williamsburg, Va.

Harper's Guest House. Mr. and Mrs. F. L. Harper have three rooms for guests in their pleasant home. Outside, there's a nice tree-shaded front yard with chairs for sitting and watching the world go by. The house, built in 1950, is furnished in antiques. Guest rooms share one bath. Morning coffee is provided, and the Harpers will gladly give you directions to restaurants, shops, etc. Colonial Williamsburg is one mile away, Busch Gardens six miles. Parking is available at the house.

GUEST HOUSES

Harper's Guest House, 724 By Pass Road, Williamsburg, VA 23185; (804) 229-1247. Rates: $12 single, $14 double. Cash, personal or traveler's checks only. No pets; children are welcome. Open year-around.

"The Cedars." A very handsome house indeed, "The Cedars" is a four-story, 200-year-old brick Georgian Colonial, with lovely grounds. Mrs. Rose deB. Harris, a gracious lady, offers guests a choice of six attractive rooms. Delightful antiques are used throughout, including canopy beds and a marvelous old sleigh bed. All the rooms have private baths and are air conditioned. Mrs. Harris invites her guests to share the sitting room and its large collection of books on Colonial architecture and biographies of prominent Colonial figures. Off-street parking for six cars is available.

In addition, there is a separate, two-story brick "Country Cottage" that accommodates six guests. The cottage has a private bath, is air conditioned and has both a Franklin stove and elec-

The Cedars, Williamsburg, Va.

tric baseboard heat. It even has a modern kitchen and laundry facilities.

The Cedars is within easy walking distance of Colonial Williamsburg; Mrs. Harris recommends visiting the shops in the restored area's Merchant Square. She does not serve food, but will be pleased to suggest some good places to eat nearby, including the excellent and very reasonably priced college cafeteria.

The Cedars, 616 Jamestown Road, Williamsburg, VA 23185; (804) 229-3591. (Opposite Phi Beta Kappa Hall, College of William and Mary.) Single $18-$20; double $22-$25; extra person in room $5 each. Family suite, two rooms with connecting bath, $42-$45. Cottage for six, $66. Cash, personal or traveler's checks accepted; no credit cards. Children are welcome; pets allowed in cottage only. Open year-around.

Hughes Guest Home. Mrs. Genevieve O. Hughes' home is furnished with "family pieces"—antiques from various periods. For travelers, she offers accommodations for singles or doubles in one room with a private bath or a suite that consists of one room with twin beds, one with a double bed and a connecting bath. There is free parking available at a lot adjacent to the house. No meals are served, but the Williamsburg Lodge offers excellent food and is only half a block away. Williamsburg's restored Colonial area is one block away.

Hughes Guest House, 106 Newport Avenue, Williamsburg, VA 23185; (804) 229-3493. (Call after 5 p.m.). Approximately $20 per room for one or two persons (plus tax). Cash or personal checks; no credit cards. No pets or children, please. Open year-around.

Whittaker's Guest House. Set amidst a grove of shade trees on a pleasant, quiet street, Ann G. Whittaker's house was built in 1965. It is a very attractive brick ranch surrounded by greenery and flowering shrubs. There are two double rooms for guests: one has a private half bath; the other (with twin beds) shares the full bath. No food is served, but there is a large Morrison's Cafeteria across the way, plus several other good restaurants within walking distance. Parking is available.

Whittaker's Guest House, 102 Thomas Nelson Lane, Williamsburg, VA 23185; (804) 229-3920. (Located in a development area called Skipwith Farms, a few minutes' drive from Colonial Williamsburg.) Reservations by phone are required. Large double room with half-bath $18 per night; twin bedroom $16 per night; plus $3 per night for a roll-away bed. Cash or personal checks only. No pets or small children. Open year-around.

Williamsburg Inn Colonial Houses. In addition to Williamsburg's large selection of guest houses, there is a unique form of accommodations called Williamsburg Inn Colonial Houses. Located in the restored Historic Area itself, they offer guest facilities in a score of Colonial homes, shops, taverns and

GUEST HOUSES

cottages; all are beautifully furnished in authentic eighteenth-century style. The buildings range from a sixteen-room brick tavern to a tiny cottage tucked away in a garden, and they are all absolutely delightful—and expensive. But staying in one is well worth the cost if you're feeling extravagant—it's like going back two hundred years in time (with all the modern conveniences). The Colonial Houses are operated by the Williamsburg Inn and receive its full services. The Inn is within easy walking distance.

For information, write to Richard W. Tate, Reservations Manager, Williamsburg Inn Colonial Houses, Williamsburg, VA 23185; (800) 446-8956. In Virginia phone (800) 582-8976; local number (804) 229-1000. Advance reservations are recommended, and a deposit of the first night's room rate is required. (Make check payable to The Colonial Williamsburg Foundation.) Rates for single or double occupancy $60-$85 per day, suites or complete houses (two to eight people) $90-$290. Personal or traveler's checks accepted; no credit cards. No pets allowed (they are accepted only at the Lodge or Motor House.) Open year-around.

The Colonial Houses Guest Cottage
Williamsburg, Va.

Hampton, Newport News, Norfolk, Portsmouth
and Virginia Beach

Southeast from Williamsburg is a cluster of seaport towns: Hampton, Newport News, Norfolk and Portsmouth. Virginia Beach is just beyond and faces the Atlantic Ocean. Venerable Hampton's history began when the Jamestown colony sent some of its men here in 1610 to cultivate the area's abundantly growing wild grapes. Although Jamestown was founded three years earlier, Hampton claims the honor of being the oldest English settlement in America *still in existence*. St. John's Church, built in 1728 as a replacement for earlier churches on the site, is the oldest continuous Episcopal parish in the nation.

To see the town and its points of interest, take the self-guided motor tour by following the red and white "Hampton Tour" signs. In addition to St. John's Church there is Kicotan Indian Village, a reproduction of a typical Indian village of the 1600s. Fort Monroe may be explored, too. Begun in 1819, it is located on the site of two earlier forts. Robert E. Lee served here, and Jefferson Davis was once imprisoned in one of the fort's casemates (a chamber in the fort walls). In 1862 the battle of the ironclads *Monitor* and *Merrimack* took place in the waters of adjacent Hampton Roads. Today Fort Monroe is the headquarters for the U.S. Army Training and Doctrine Command. This richly historic fort is well worth seeing.

Newport News, Norfolk and Portsmouth make up the Port of Hampton Roads, one of the world's finest natural harbors. If you have the time, take a harbor cruise from any one of the three towns to see some of the area's vast shipping and shipbuilding operations. The Museum in Newport News offers a fascinating collection of such nautical articles as ship models, figureheads, paintings and prints.

In Norfolk travelers may tour the Naval Base and visit the General Douglas MacArthur Memorial's galleries of memorabilia. The Chrysler Museum contains a stunning collection of Titians, Renoirs and other masterpieces. For some fresh-air sight-seeing, try the lovely Norfolk Botanical Gardens or Lafayette Zoo. Portsmouth (connected with Norfolk by tunnels and bridges) is famed for its fine old historic houses. It also has the Naval Shipyard Museum, which contains an enormous number of nautical artifacts.

Virginia's Dismal Swamp (a fairly apt name) lies a bit south of the Portsmouth/Norfolk area. This eerie swamp stretches for

GUEST HOUSES

about 40 miles in a long, narrow ribbon of trembling peat. Lake Drummond in its center, reachable by boat, is an 18-square-mile expanse of amber-colored water. Because the lake's water retained its sweet freshness for so long, it was once highly prized for use aboard ships.

For sun and saltwater fun, Virginia Beach (just east of Portsmouth) offers 28 miles of fabulous white sand beach, great swimming and fishing and a host of other sports activities and amusements. It also has two excellent guest houses.

Angie's Guest Cottage. Located right in the heart of Virginia Beach, Angie's Guest Cottage has a fine view of the ocean from its sun deck. Bob and Barbara Yates Royster and Barbara's parents, Bob and Garnette Yates, operate the place. Accommodations include four single and/or double rooms, one triple room, and one room that sleeps four or five. There are also two apartments that sleep up to four comfortably. Five rooms share two centrally located baths; one room has a private bath (as do

Angies Guest House, Virgina Beach, Va.

both apartments).

The rooms and apartments are all decorated to make guests feel right at home. One room opens directly onto the sun deck. All have good, firm beds and are air conditioned; some have small refrigerators for snacks and cold drinks. Television sets are available upon request. The apartments are large efficiencies with eat-in kitchens and full-size appliances. Coffee pot, toaster, dishes and cookware are all included. Parking is available in the driveway and on the street.

In addition to the sun deck, there is a nice front porch for just sitting and people-watching and a fenced-in backyard with barbecue pit and picnic tables. During the summer the Roysters and Yates hold frequent cookouts featuring hotdogs, hamburgers and crabs—and all guests are invited! The atmosphere at Angie's is delightfully friendly, warm and family-style.

The house is one short block from the beach, and one and a half hours' drive from Colonial Williamsburg. Your hosts will gladly tell you about all the interesting sights and activities in the Virginia Beach/Norfolk/Portsmouth area, including tips on the best restaurants. No food is served, except for those occasional cookouts. And Barbara Royster says: "Thank goodness—I'm allergic to the kitchen!"

Angie's Guest Cottage, 302 24th Street, Virginia Beach, VA 23451; (804) 428-8052 or 428-4690. (Located at the intersection of Twenty-fourth Street and Pacific Avenue. The house is eleven miles from the exit of the Chesapeake Bay Bridge Tunnel, Rte. 13, and two blocks from Rte. 44. The Greyhound Bus Station is just across the way; the house is also on the public bus line.) In general, in-season rates (Memorial Day to Labor Day) are: single $18-$25, double $22-$30, room with private bath (for two, three or four persons) $32-$40, apartments $40-$45. Off season: single $10-$16, double $12-$22, room with private bath $18-$26, apartments $25-$30. Both in-and off-season rates are lowered slightly at certain times of the year, such as in early June and in December, and low weekly rates are also available. Cash or traveler's checks, MasterCard and Visa accepted; no personal checks. Small pets and well-behaved children are welcome. Open year-around.

The Sinclair. A large, comfortable beach house, the Sinclair is owned and operated by Darlene Thurman and Ron McInturff. It is a pleasant, cheerful establishment, done up in early-American style. There are twenty-five guest rooms, fifteen with shared baths and ten with private baths. All rooms are air condi-

The Sinclair, Virginia Beach, Va.

tioned, and there are connecting rooms for families.

Guests are invited to enjoy the pleasant television lounge or relax on the oceanfront verandas. There is parking on the premises, and 24-hour switchboard service. Baby-sitters are available, on request. No food is served; ask your friendly hosts for suggestions on the best places to eat in the vicinity. They will also give directions to shops, golf courses, tennis courts and good fishing piers.

The Sinclair, 2607 Atlantic Avenue, Virginia Beach, VA 23451; (804) 428-4733. (On the oceanfront at Twenty-sixth Street.) Rates: rooms with connecting bath $28-$32, with private bath $32-$36; rooms facing the ocean $36-$42. Traveler's checks, cash, Visa and MasterCard accepted. No pets, please; children welcome. Open April 1 to October 31.

THE EASTERN SHORE

When the first settlers arrived on the Eastern Shore peninsula in 1614, they kept its Indian name, *Accawmacke* ("Land beyond the waters"). It was a very different world from the Tidewater's baronial plantations and aristocratic way of life. The inhabitants of the Eastern Shore led a simpler existence; they fished and farmed and built small villages much like those on Massachusetts' Cape Cod.

Life on the Eastern Shore has changed little over the centuries. Fishing and farming are still major occupations; the picturesque towns are still Colonial in appearance and character.

The region's windswept beaches and sandy barrier islands, too, seem to resist the passage of time. This tranquil, unhurried place has wonderful swimming and fishing and some of the finest seafood in the world.

To reach the Eastern Shore from Virginia Beach or Norfolk, follow the blue and white signs marked with a sea gull to the Chesapeake Bay Bridge Tunnel. A 17.6-mile stretch of road, the impressive highway runs through two mile-long tunnels, over 12 miles of trestled roadway and 2 miles of causeway, two long bridges and four man-made islands. It is an engineering marvel, and an awesomely scenic drive.

Up at the northern end of the peninsula are the islands of Assateague and Chincoteague. Assateague contains both the Virginia portion of the Assateague Island National Seashore and the Chincoteague National Wildlife Refuge. It is also the home of those famous wild ponies described so charmingly in Marguerite Henry's book, *Misty of Chincoteague.*

According to legend, the ponies first came to Assateague about 400 years ago, swimming ashore from the wreck of a Spanish galleon. Every July some of the residents of Chincoteague Island round up the ponies and swim them across the channel for "penning." The ensuing week-long festival has pony rides, carnivals, delicious Chincoteague oysters and freshly caught crabs and clams to eat and an auction in which the wild pony foals are sold. The remaining ponies swim back to Assateague, where they are allowed to roam freely the rest of the year. Actually, they are not ponies, but stunted horses, their size having dwindled over the years from a diet of marsh grass. When the horses are young, they are about the size of a large dog; when full-grown they resemble large Shetlands.

Year of the Horse Inn. During the annual roundup, the Assateague ponies are paraded right past this delightful guest house! Owned by Carlton and Jean Bond, the Year of the Horse is located on Chincoteague Island, overlooking Chincoteague Bay. It is only a block from the carnival grounds, and private parking is available on the premises.

The older part of the house is 60 years old; the guest rooms are, as Jean Bond puts it, "Six years young." They are all large and air conditioned and have cable television, private baths and balconies. There is an efficiency with two double beds, a room with queen-size bed and a private two-bedroom apartment. Guests are also invited to use the lobby with its interesting collection of antiques and contemporary pieces that combine to give a "Sidney Greenstreet" ambiance.

Outdoors there is a picnic area and a private pier. The former owner of the house had a pony named Cloudy, grandson of the beloved Misty. On one occasion, Cloudy and the famous television horse-star, Mr. Ed, went swimming off the pier. Mr. Ed then performed tricks for all the children who had gathered to watch.

No meals are served at The Year of the Horse, but the Bonds own a restaurant conveniently nearby, which specializes in fresh seafood. The house is also close to the Assateague National Wildlife Refuge with its superb beaches, the Atlantic Ocean, hiking and biking trails, birds galore and those wonderful wild ponies. The fishing is great, too. Chincoteague, in addition to all of its other attractions, is known as the flounder fishing capital of the world.

Year of the Horse Inn, 600 S. Main Street, Chincoteague Island, VA 23336; (804) 336-3221. Large efficiency with two double beds: March through April $30; May through June $32; July through Labor Day $36; September $32; October and November $30. Large room with queen-size bed, $6 less than efficiency. Private two-bedroom apartment (three-night limit) $36 per night. Rates are based on double occupancy. Each extra person in room $4; one or two children under ten years of age free. Lower rates in winter months. One day's deposit required on reservation. Personal checks or cash, Visa or MasterCard accepted. Check-in time is 1 p.m.; check-out 11 a.m. No pets, please. Open year-around.

Tangier Island, in Chesapeake Bay west of the Eastern Shore, is still inhabited by the descendants of its original seventeenth-century settlers. Many of its residents still make their livings by fishing and the community is almost untouched by modern concerns. Some of the natives even speak with an Old English accent. Reaching the island is not a simple matter of driving across a bridge; it is accessible in the summer months via excursion boats from Reedville, Virginia, across the Bay, or from Crisfield, Maryland. In wintertime, the Crisfield boat is the only one available. From the Eastern Shore, drive a few miles north on U.S. 13 to Pocomoke City in Maryland, then take Rts. 667 and 413 down to Crisfield.

Mrs. Euna Dise/Guest House. Mrs. Dise's guest house has no name; as she says, everyone on the island knows everyone else so she does not need one! Her comfortable two-and-a-half-story home with porches in front and back has three rooms for guests—one with a double bed and single bed and two with a double bed. The rooms share one bath. Rates are incredibly reasonable, only six dollars per person.

Mrs. Dise welcomes visitors all year around, but cautions that the winter months can get a bit nippy. If you do come in the off-season, please note that the boat from Maryland leaves every day at 12:30 p.m.; the boat from Tangier Island back to Maryland departs at 8 a.m. Be sure to call or write Mrs. Dise ahead of time for reservations and instructions on how to reach her house. The house is within walking distance of the landing, but Mrs. Dise will meet you at the boat if you wish.

Mrs. Dise does not serve meals. She does, however, provide morning coffee for her guests at 25 cents a cup. The Chesapeake House nearby is a good place to eat, and your hostess will be happy to suggest others.

Mrs. Euna Dise/Guest House, Box 24, Tangier Island, VA 23440; (804) 891-2425. Six dollars per night, cash only accepted. Open year-around.

VIRGINIA'S MOUNTAINS
AND THE SHENANDOAH VALLEY

The Blue Ridge Mountains of Virginia lie just west of the state's central Piedmont Plateau. Beyond them stretches the Great Valley, which separates the Blue Ridge from the Allegheny range. There are actually five valleys; the Shenandoah, through which flows the beautiful Shenandoah River, is the northernmost. During the Civil War the lovely, fertile Shenandoah Valley became a bloody battlefield, fought over time and time again by the opposing armies. Let's begin our exploration of the region up at the top of the valley, at the historic town of Winchester.

Winchester

Once a Shawnee Indian camping ground, Winchester was first settled in 1732 by a group of Pennsylvania Quakers. In 1748 Thomas, Lord Fairfax, hired the young George Washington to survey some land in the area. Washington spent three years at the job, working out of an office in the town. By the Civil War years, Winchester was an important transportation center; it became a prize of great value to both Northern and Southern forces. The town changed hands more than seventy times (thirteen times, it is said, in one day), and some six battles and more than 100 minor skirmishes were fought in the vicinity.

Today, Winchester is the center of Virginia's apple-growing region and home of the Shenandoah Apple Blossom Festival, held each May. An auto tour of the town leads to several historic cemeteries and churches; General "Stonewall" Jackson's Headquarters where he lived during the winter of 1861-1862; General Philip H. Sheridan's Headquarters (during the fall and winter of 1864-1865); and George Washington's Office, which now houses a museum.

Ramsburg's Guest House. Mrs. James B. Yates is your gracious hostess at this nice old Colonial-style home in Winchester. The house, which has a wide porch running most of the way around, has been in the family for three generations. It was built in 1917 by Mrs. Yates' grandfather. There are four double rooms for guests (with one double bed), two rooms with two double beds, and two baths (one semi-private). All of the rooms are tastefully decorated, very comfortable and extremely reasonable in price. Parking is available at the house. Restaurants, shops and many of Winchester's historic sites are within walking distance. General Jackson's Headquarters are

Ramsburg's Guest House, Winchester, Va.

only half a block away.

Ramsburg's Guest House, 31 Peyton Street, Winchester, VA 22601; (703) 662-3114. (Corner of Peyton and Braddock Streets. Braddock is also Rte. 11 South.) Single $7.50; double $12; three in room $15; four in room $18; all plus 4 percent sales tax. Cash only accepted, no credit cards or checks. Children and well-behaved pets are welcome. Open year-around.

Charlottesville

Virginia's famed Skyline Drive begins about 19 miles south of Winchester, at Front Royal. The drive winds for 105 spectacular miles through Shenandoah National Park and should not be missed. It follows along the crest of the Blue Ridge Mountains, twisting and curving in gentle grades, marked by tumbling waterfalls and frequent overlooks. Travelers may stop to hike, ride horseback, picnic or fish along the way. Two handsome lodges offer traditional Southern food and a breathtaking view. Mountain craft gift shops at the lodges contain a wide variety of such handmade items as pottery, basketwork, wrought iron, wooden toys and handwoven skirts and bedspreads.

Skyline Drive comes to an end at Rockfish Gap between Waynesboro and Charlottesville, but there the magnificent Blue Ridge Parkway begins. The parkway follows the mountains for 469 miles all the way to North Carolina's Great Smoky Mountains National Park. Both the Skyline Drive and Blue Ridge Parkway are driveable all year except for brief periods in the winter when occasional fog or ice closes them down. They are especially glorious in the spring when apple trees, dogwood and rhododendron are in bloom and again in the fall when the mountainsides blaze in a flaming tapestry of color.

This section of Virginia, along with its countless other attractions, offers a number of fascinating caverns for visitors to explore. Luray Caverns on U.S. 211, ten minutes from the Skyline's central entrance, are the largest caverns in eastern America. It has been said that if you've seen one cave you've seen them all, but Luray's underground marvels are really impressive—and vast. Wear comfortable shoes, as you will be doing a lot of walking. Carry a sweater; the caverns are damp and chilly. And remember: stalactites grow downward, stalagmites grow upward.

Charlottesville, at the end of the Skyline Drive, is an ideal place to stop and stay for a day or so. Set in the rolling hills below the Blue Ridge Mountains, it is Thomas Jefferson's hometown and the site of his handsome mansion, Monticello.

GUEST HOUSES

Jefferson began building the house in 1769; it took 40 years to complete. Perched atop a small mountain, the graciously classical structure is surrounded by charming gardens.

The house, which actually has 35 rooms, seems deceptively small from the front. Jefferson created this effect by designing the second-story windows to appear to be part of those on the ground-floor level. And instead of following the custom of the time by constructing separate outbuildings for servants, supplies and various functions, he included a complex of twelve concealed underground rooms for those purposes.

Jefferson believed in labor-saving devices, too, and Monticello is full of them. There are glass double doors that swing open in unison when either is opened; they are operated by a system of hidden chains. A wall panel in the dining room is a revolving buffet; servants would load it from outside with dishes from the kitchens below. Dumbwaiters concealed in the mantelpiece brought wine from the cellar. And these are only a few of the countless innovations incorporated into the house.

An awesomely knowledgeable man, Jefferson was a Renaissance American—with an interest in virtually every subject. His brilliance was wittily described by President John F. Kennedy some years ago at a dinner for a group of Nobel laureates. Kennedy praised his guests as "the most extraordinary collection of talents . . . that has ever gathered together at the White House, with the possible exception of when Thomas Jefferson dined alone." Jefferson died at Monticello on July 4, 1826, exactly fifty years after the signing of the Declaration of Independence. His home is open to visitors daily except Christmas.

After exploring Monticello, take a walk around the University of Virginia's grounds; their beautiful brick buildings and walls are further examples of Jefferson's architectural genius. Ash Lawn, located five miles southeast of Charlottesville, is another. Jefferson planned the house and its gardens for James Monroe in 1798.

Venable Guest House. While in Charlottesville, you are invited to stay at Mr. and Mrs. Robert Stewart's pleasant 70-year-old brick home, the Venable Guest House. The Stewarts offer guests a choice of seven rooms at very reasonable rates; three of the rooms have twin beds and four have double beds. One bath is shared by two rooms, another by five. Several of the rooms are decorated in antiques. The house is only two blocks from the University campus, 15 minutes from Monticello and 20 minutes from Ash Lawn. Shops and several good restaurants are within easy walking distance. The Stewarts do not serve meals, but there is a refrigerator available for guests to use for snacks and soft drinks. On-street parking is available.

Venable Guest House, 316 Fourteenth Street N.W., Charlottesville, VA 22903; (804) 295-7707. (Close to I-64 and Rte. 29.) Single $12.50; double $14.50; both plus tax. Cots are available for $2 extra. Cash or personal checks are accepted; no credit cards. No pets, please. Open year-around.

Guesthouses, Bed & Breakfast. Guesthouses is an organization that arranges lodgings (not otherwise advertised) in a number of private homes in the Charlottesville area, offering a wide variety of accommodations. Mrs. Sally Reger, manager of this useful service, has some forty choices available; most of them include a Continental breakfast in the rates. The accommodations range from exclusive country estates and cottages to apartment efficiencies near the University of Virginia in town, with as many individual touches and amenities as there are house-owners—cozy fireplaces, flowers and fruit in the room and lots more.

Mrs. Reger says that the majority of her listings are the homes of professional people who find Guesthouses an excellent opportunity to meet interesting people from all over the world. They all offer high quality (often elegant) lodgings; several of the homes have been included on house and garden tours in recent years. The average rate for an overnight stay runs between $26 and $36 per couple. Some especially outstanding accommodations are more expensive; others will be less. Singles, efficiencies and weekly rates are also available. Mrs. Reger will provide full details and help choose just the right place for you, depending upon the kind of bed you want, private or shared bath, breakfast or complete cooking facilities and location.

Mrs. Sally Reger, Manager, Guesthouses/Bed & Breakfast, P.O. Box 5737, Charlottesville, VA 22903; (804) 973-7403. (Phone 1 p.m.-6 p.m., Monday through Friday.) Advance notice is required by phone, followed by a deposit of $25 or the first night's lodging charge if you plan to stay more than one night. The deposit is refundable in part if cancellation notice is received within 48 hours of the intended arrival time. If time permits, Mrs. Reger will mail confirmation of reservation along with a map of Charlottesville. She will also include sight-seeing folders and a list of restaurants, if they are requested.

GUEST HOUSES

Lexington

Down Virginia's mountain chain on the Blue Ridge Parkway, about 50 miles southwest of Charlottesville is the turn-off for Lexington. This charming, historic town is home of the prestigious Virginia Military Institute (1839) and Washington and Lee University, founded in 1749. Confederate generals Robert E. Lee and Thomas J. "Stonewall" Jackson are both buried here. Several interesting tours may be followed; one covers some of the highlights of Lee's and Jackson's lives, and another leads through the grounds of the Virginia Military Institute. A third, the Residential Walking Tour, encompasses Lexington's newly restored downtown area and some 24 historic homes. Information and brochures on all of these may be acquired at the Visitor Information Center, 107 East Washington Street.

The Alexander-Withrow House. A Virginia Historic Landmark, this lovely old house was built in 1789 and has been completely restored and furnished in authentic period style. Located in the center of Old Lexington near the campuses of Washington and Lee and V.M.I., the house offers six elegant suites for overnight guests.

Four of the suites include a living room with double hide-a-bed and refreshment center, a large bedroom with double bed and private bath. An attic suite, ideal for families, has two bedrooms and two full baths; a ground floor suite also has two baths, bedroom, sitting room and living room. All suites have central heating, air conditioning and private telephone. Daily maid service is included. Among the furnishings are antiques and period reproductions, books, paintings and prints and an attractive touch of greenery provided by potted plants.

Mrs. Beth Bradford manages the Alexander-Withrow House; she also operates a small general bookstore located on the ground floor. The house is a handsome structure of stone and brick and has a first-floor lobby where antiques and handcrafted items are for sale. Alongside the house, a narrow passageway has been converted into a delightful brick-paved courtyard, which guests are invited to use during the warmer months. No meals are served, but Mrs. Bradford will be happy to suggest a few of Lexington's fine restaurants. Ask her, too, to relate the history of the house and its several incarnations as a post office, school, bank and shop.

Alexander-Withrow House, 3 West Washington Street, Lexington, VA

24450; (703) 463-2044. (Corner of Main and Washington Streets.) Rates average $40 per person, plus $5 for each additional occupant. MasterCard and Visa accepted. No pets, please. Open year-around.

Lynchburg

Before leaving the Lexington area, take a drive 13 miles south on U.S. 11 and see Virginia's Natural Bridge. It is a massive 215-foot-high limestone arch, 90 feet long and widening to 150 feet in some places. Its span joins two mountains, and the highway runs right over it. Long ago, Indians worshipped the bridge; in 1750 George Washington cut his initials in it; and in 1774 Thomas Jefferson was so taken by the stone arch that he bought it! Jefferson paid King George III of England twenty shillings for the bridge, gorge and all, then hired caretakers and built a visitor's cabin nearby. During the American Revolution the bridge was used as a shot tower; molten lead was dropped from the top of the span into the creek below to make bullets for Washington's armies. The Natural Bridge may be visited daily from 7 a.m. to dark; nightly there is a drama with lights and music, which tells the story of the Creation.

Civil War history buffs will want to visit the Appomatox Court House National Historic Park. From the Blue Ridge Parkway southeast of Lexington, take U.S. 501 down to Lynchburg, and then U.S. 460 East. The Appomatox Court House Building houses a visitor center and museum, and offers an audiovisual slide program. From there you can take a self-guided tour to such various sites as the Clover Hill Tavern, Lee's and Grant's headquarters, the old County Jail, and McLean House—where, on April 9, 1865, General Robert E. Lee surrendered to General Ulysses S. Grant and ended the Civil War. The park is open all year except for Christmas Day.

Scott's Tourist Home. Located in Lynchburg, this large guest house is owned and operated by Lawrence and Rose Scott. They have ten nicely priced rooms; eight have double beds, and two have two double beds and extra cots. Three baths are shared. No meals are served, but guests may fix their own meals in the kitchen if they like. If not, there are restaurants within walking distance. Parking is available.
Scott's Tourist Home, 717 Madison Street, Lynchburg, VA 24504; (804) 528-9348. (On the corner of Madison and Eighth Streets.) Basement room $10.30; upstairs rooms with shared bath $11.33, with private bath $13.39; rooms with two double beds $16.48. Weekly rates are available.

GUEST HOUSES

Cash only; no credit cards or checks. Pets and children accepted. Open year-around.

From Lynchburg, travelers may follow the Blue Ridge Parkway down into North Carolina or take some time and head over into Virginia's rugged southwest Highlands. The Highlands are densely forested land with icy mountain lakes and streams. Parks galore offer great fishing, hunting, camping and countless miles of trails.

At Big Stone Gap, summertime visitors may watch an exciting drama called *The Trail of the Lonesome Pine*. It is an outdoor musical version of John Fox's classic novel about life in the Highlands. And there is the famed Barter Theatre in Abingdon, now the State Theatre of Virginia. Robert Porterfield, a Virginia native, came home to these mountains during the Depression in the 1930s and brought with him a troupe of Broadway artists who acted in return for hams, vegetables, homemade jam—whatever the people had to offer.

Finally, trace your way to Cumberland Gap, where you can stand with one foot in Virginia and the other in Kentucky, and from a look-out see into Virginia, Kentucky, North Carolina and Tennessee.

Index of Guest Houses

GUEST HOUSES

About the Author

Corinne Madden Ross, a free-lance writer living near Boston, stays in guest houses whenever possible on her many travels. She has published numerous travel articles and is author of the prize-winning **Christmas In Scandinavia** (1977) and **To Market, To Market: Six Walking Tours of the Old & the New Boston** (1980).

She is also the author of **The New England Guest House Book** (East Woods Press, 1979) and the co-author of the forthcoming **New England: Off the Beaten Path** (East Woods Press, 1981).

don't miss . . .

The Grand Strand: An Uncommon Guide to Myrtle Beach and its Surroundings. Nancy Rhyne. A wealth of historical and unusual information about this popular vacation area.

Just Folks: Visitin' With Carolina People. Jerry Bledsoe. Charles Kuralt calls Jerry "Carolina's Listener Laureate" with this collection of "conversations" with 66 fascinating North and South Carolinians.

Sea Islands of the South. Diana and Bill Gleasner. A beautifully photographed and well-written guide to the exquisite coastal islands of North Carolina, South Carolina, Georgia and Florida.

and others . . .

Backcountry Cooking by J. Wayne Fears
The Complete Guide to Backpacking in Canada
   by Elliott Katz
Florida By Paddle and Pack by Mike Toner and Pat Toner
The Fructose Cookbook by Minuha Cannon
The Healthy Trail Food Book by Dorcas S. Miller
Honky Tonkin' by Richard Wooton
Hosteling USA by Michael Frome
Inside Outward Bound by Renate Wilson
The Living Land by Marguerite Schumann
The Maine Coast by Dorcas S. Miller
New England: Off the Beaten Path
   by Corinne MaddenRoss and Ralph Woodward
Steppin' Out by Susanne Weil and Barry Singer
Sweets Without Guilt by Minuha Cannon
Train Trips by William G. Scheller
Trout Fishing the Southern Appalachians by J. Wayne Fears
A Vacationer's Guide to Orlando and Central Florida
   by Judi Foster Grove
Walks With Nature in Rocky Mountain National Park
   by Kent and Donna Dannen
Wild Places of the South by Steve Price
You Can't Live On Radishes by Jerry Bledsoe

The East Woods Press
820 East Boulevard
Charlotte, NC 28203